WITHDRAWN

D1158343

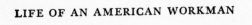
LIFE OF AN AMERICAN WORKMAN

926
C468l

LIFE OF
AN AMERICAN
WORKMAN

BY

WALTER P. CHRYSLER

IN COLLABORATION WITH

BOYDEN SPARKES

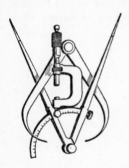

DODD, MEAD & COMPANY · NEW YORK

Copyright, 1937, by THE CURTIS PUBLISHING COMPANY

Copyright, 1950, by WALTER P. CHRYSLER, JR., JACK CHRYSLER,
THELMA CHRYSLER FOY AND BERNICE CHRYSLER GARBISCH

ALL RIGHTS RESERVED
NO PART OF THIS BOOK MAY BE REPRODUCED IN ANY FORM
WITHOUT PERMISSION IN WRITING FROM THE PUBLISHER

PRINTED IN THE UNITED STATES OF AMERICA
BY THE AMERICAN BOOK–KNICKERBOCKER PRESS, INC., N. Y.

TO

DELLA

100618

PREFACE

GREAT things are implicit in the life of Walter P. Chrysler. Outstanding and unusual though it was, his narrative reflects the lives of so many other American workmen, born not to wealth but to the wholesome discipline and chores of household and farm—men who by work, hardships and accomplishment earned every step of their rise in industry and in public esteem.

In the last half century of modern industry, Mr. Chrysler personified those traditional American qualities of initiative, integrity, courage, leadership, and resourcefulness, that, in the earlier days of the republic made our people free and laid the foundation for our country's greatness.

An individualist in imagination, in energy, in personal capacity, ability, and attainment, Mr. Chrysler nevertheless believed above all in the dignity of work and the fundamental necessity for organization and team work. He selected his teammates with care. His friendship for them and his loyalty to them has been an inspiration. He inspired them with his own profound belief in an idea that is uniquely American— the idea on which his own company was built—the idea of always seeking to improve things that people need and want.

Whatever may be the individual achievements of those who read Mr. Chrysler's life, as long as opportunity—the doorway he could enter so confidently—remains a vital part of our heritage, this country will continue to be the land we wish our children and grandchildren to cherish.

K. T. KELLER

CONTENTS

· I ·

BACKGROUND OF MY BOYHOOD

1881

"You Had To Be a Tough Kid"

· I ·

BACKGROUND OF MY
BOYHOOD

BEING a machinist, I have always wanted to know how things work. A machine enabled my pioneering father and mother to provide for me; it was a steam locomotive of which my father was the engineer. All my training, instincts and aptitudes have combined to make me want to penetrate the workings of any machines I see.

Curiously, my earliest recollection of being alive is involved with an adventure growing out of the resentment of certain Americans against machines—railroad machines, and all they portended.

With a German-fairy-story fancifulness, my mother enlisted me in the service of the brass lamp in our kitchen that had its own wall shelf to roost upon. She made it seem a living thing, that lamp whose smoked-up chimney gave her a daily cleaning chore.

"You must go to the store," she told the barefooted child who nagged her for a slice of bread with sugar on it; that was me between five and six years old. "The lamp is empty and, therefore, hungry—just like you. We must give his wick a big drink or he will sulk and keep us in darkness tonight. You take this can and get some coal oil."

A withered, blackened potato was impaled upon the oil-can

spout. Ours would get a fresh potato for his nose once a month, when our account would be squared at the store on payday.

What I wore that day was a gingham shirt and a little pair of jeans-cloth pants that buttoned to it. The empty oil can clanged musically as now and then a flowering weed swished against its emptiness. We lived on the south side of the tracks; the stores, the saloons and other excitements were on the north side of the tracks. Ellis, Kansas, the railroad town where we lived, was in the heart of the short-grass country.

Two utterly different streams of life bisected each other in the vicinity of our small, isolated community; east and west ran the railroad, and its tracks bridged the creek that slanted across the prairie. This creek was a yellow thread of wilderness at the edge of town. If the railroad and its attendant establishments represented the excitements of the tame world far to the east, the stream was sometimes a murmuring reminder of other kinds of excitement. Throughout my early years there were being freshly printed in the soft banks of that stream the tracks of wild animals of the prairie by which we were surrounded—of buffalo and antelope, and of coyotes. Sometimes there were tracks of a creature that wore moccasins, a creature that hated the railroad.

You had to be a tough kid. Out there where I grew up, if you were soft, all the other kids would beat the daylights out of you. Consequently you grew tough in all your sensitive parts, just as your bare feet did in order to avoid the pain of splinters, stone bruises and rude boot heels. Nevertheless, there was one valid, scalp-raising fear in my early life which has completely lost touch with current realities. When I have spoken of it, my children have seemed incredulous. Yet history is on the side of my memory when I say that along that narrow fringe of plains civilization where we grew up, everybody lived in fear of Indians.

I was a year old when, to the north of us, Custer and his men were massacred. In the fall of 1878, when I was three and a half years old, a band of Northern Cheyennes, led by Chief Dull Knife, slaughtered some white people living on Sappa Creek and Beaver Creek, in Decatur and Rawlins counties. Other things had happened, were happening and were told of over and over in the nighttime glow around our kitchen stove, while neighbors sat and blew upon their steaming coffee poured in saucers. A Kansas white woman, when carried off by Indians, had written pleas for help on scraps of paper with which she made a trail for rescuers to follow. Why, so often did we hear the tale I almost seemed to see that despairing woman tearing paper and even her apron into scraps. Though adult voices were lowered to discuss her plight, only a dumb kid would fail to get better than a glimmering of an understanding as to why the Indians saved the women and girls, although invariably scalping men and boys. At five I was a paleface vulnerable to scalping, and knew it.

On that day, as I went for coal oil toward the railroad tracks and the stores, I saw another boy running; he cleared the tracks and headed toward me along the path. As we passed I flung a question at him.

"Indians!" he yelled. "Indians are coming!"

Right now I take a lot of credit to myself, because I did not drop the oil can as I scooted for home, clearing tufts of buffalo grass at just about the height of a prairie chicken when it flies for fresh cover. I still had the clanging oil can as I panted into our yard, yipped a warning to my mother and scrambled out of sight, down a flight of earthen steps into the moldy darkness of our cyclone cellar.

My memory of that occurrence ends as abruptly as a picture that is torn across, but another recollection which may be a piece of it begins with my small self seated on the floor, amid the smell of dust, against the wall of the second floor of the stone railroad station in Ellis; this was also the hotel. Many people were there. The women, with shawls and sun-bonnets on their heads, were enjoying the excitement of being frightened, if I can trust what I seem to remember.

Just to prove that we were in danger, the children were not allowed to play or make any noise. Every man who showed himself carried some kind of weapon; most had rifles, but a few younger men made savage gestures with axes and whiffletrees. I remember one naked saber carried almost like a doll baby in the folded arms of an old man who leaned against the wall close to me. There was stable manure on his wrinkled black boots. That occasion was certainly one of our Indian scares. I think this was in 1880; it might have been in '81. However, the Indians never got me, in keeping with my mother's promise that they never would; she would reassure me whenever I hesitated to invade, alone, the awful blackness of the bedroom. Sometimes she tucked me in, not always.

Frontier hardships accounted for great changes in the lovely Missouri-born girl with peach-bloom complexion, tender mouth and youthful form whom my father married in 1871. She was a shapely bride when she left the comfortable German culture of her father's Missouri farmhouse. By the time I became conscious of my dependence on her, my mother's large dark eyes were set in a big powerful woman of the frontier. I was the third of four children she bore in Kansas railroad towns in the 70's before the prairies had been tamed. She ate buffalo meat to nourish her sons. Sometimes now I seem to see her eyes looking at me, miraculously, out of the face of one of my grandchildren. Sometimes, in a mirror, I catch a fleeting trace of her in my own eyes. At such times I hope afresh that they were right, those vanished Ellis neighbors who, when drinking coffee in our kitchen, would cast a nod at me and say, "Walt takes after his ma."

Work? Of course, a boy had to work in a household where my mother was the ruler. She worked all the time herself and had prodigious energy. What awakened me every day was the clangor of iron lids on her cookstove before the sun was up. For years her kitchen fire was the only heat we knew in winter, and to reach its blazing comfort in a morning that was still night-black, often I had to scamper bare-footed across a floor where snow had drifted through the cracks of badly fitting windows. I shared a bed with my bigger brother Ed, who was three years and three months older. Before breakfast Ed had cows to milk, but I had other work to do.

Sometimes I was sent early to get the soup meat. Until I was six or seven, the few hundred people who lived in Ellis almost never got beef; we all ate buffalo meat. There was an abundance of it and it was cheap; some of it was shipped east to other towns. The rump was what my mother wanted. She would put a great hunk of this maroon-and-bluish gristled meat into the big black iron pot in which she made her soup. I have never tasted any other soup quite so good. She never served her soup on the day she made it, but, steaming hot, it would appear on the table the next morning when we had breakfast. What enormous meals those were with which a Kansas day began back in the '80's! Steaks, potatoes, pancakes, followed soup. Often we had hominy, but if we did, we owed it, every grain, to my mother. She soaked the yellow grains in lye water until the flintlike yellow coating vanished. A mound of hominy was material out of which to build a dike to retain a lake of gravy. My mother not only made the hominy but she grew the corn. She had a garden where no weed was ever tolerated. There was no task she ever dodged for lack of strength or skill or willingness.

15

A certain soft scraping sound that I hear faintly sometimes in a barbershop is like an echo of a harsh and loud scrape, scrape, scrape that I used to hear in our kitchen when I was a boy. As I listen, with my face and mind erased of present things by a barber's soothing towel, I doze; and, dozing, slip back to one of those moments of my past that is quickened by the razor's noise. Our kitchen was the only barbershop my father knew. My mother was the one who always cut his hair and shaved him. We never spent money for anything that we could get without spending.

When it happened on a Sunday morning, the shaving of my father was a part of the family preparation for attendance at church services. His upper lip, by design and in accordance with the prevailing masculine fashion of the West, was always black with a thick glossy mustache that drooped at the corners of his mouth. That was proper, but the stubbly growth of whiskers on his cheeks, neck and chin was as disturbing to my mother, as little to be tolerated, as weeds in her kitchen garden. So, badgered by her, my father would seat himself midway between the window and the stove, on which a basin of water would be steaming. I have forgotten how the lather brush had been improvised, but I never can forget that the soap, often with my conscripted labor, was home-made out of grease and lye. With a prod of her thumb against the bristles of his chin, my mother would tilt his head and give him an iridescent beard of bubbles. When this had become foamy, she would start to scrape.

You can bet my father's skin was tough! It had to be to withstand that kind of homemade soap, along with Kansas sun and wind and blizzards. But if his skin was like bristly leather, his heart was gentle. We two boys, his sons, were a pair of fighting chore-dodging cubs, unruly and frequently in need of taming; yet he never laid a hand on us in anger. He

16

would reason with us and get obedience, but his mighty arms and calloused hands were never used against us. In many of the visions of him that recur to me, there is a paintbrush in his hand, or a hammer or a saw. Always he was trying to make life better for his family. Our first Ellis house—the first of three—was of the plainest kind. It was badly put together and, in winter, through its cracks, the snow intruded. It had a little porch, though, and two bedrooms beside the combination kitchen-dining-living room. A railroad shanty? Oh, no. It was Hank Chrysler's home, a house to swell my mother's heart with pride as she showed it off to neighbors who still were living half buried in the prairie earth in houses made of sod.

We were lucky. Because my father worked for the railroad, we were privileged to buy some of its coal when certain other folks in Ellis had no fuel except the dried dung of buffalo or cows. Out hunting, I've warmed my hands over a quick-burning fire of cow chips, oh, many a time, when my fingers got too numb to feel a shotgun trigger. But at home we had a shed full of coal to burn, along with kindling that my brother Ed and I were required to find and cut. When we neglected this, or when we disobeyed her slightest order, our mother spanked us. The mace of her authority was a hairbrush. Corporal punishment? When my mother flailed me on my rear, it seemed to be inflicted by a major general at least. Once, against my private person, that hairbrush was jarred from all its bristles, but it was kept in spanking service until I was nearly seventeen. I was not docile then, or ever, but my mother had the strength to put me, big as I was, across her knee and spank me until my roars convinced her that I was blushing in my pants and improved in my intentions.

My father and mother were a great pair of people; hard-

17

working partners devoted to the job of bringing up a family.

My mother's pumpkin pies were famous out in Ellis, but Henry Chrysler was known, I guess, from end to end of the Union Pacific. Certainly he was the best locomotive engineer on the division. When the railroad bought its first coal-burning locomotive, he was the engineer chosen to leave the cab of a wood burner and take command of that grand mechanism that snorted in an even cadence when it went puff, puff, puff, puffing eastward out of Ellis at 7:30 in the morning. I used to watch him then and still be thinking of him when I got to school at eight o'clock.

Often when he left the house I walked beside him, lugging his dinner pail. What he carried rested on his hip—a great big six-shooter that sagged below his coat. It had a black butt of a size to fill his fist. When I was ten, the handle of that weapon hung on my father just at the level of my stubbly, home-cut hair, above my eager eyes. I always called him papa. He was no swashbuckler, just a railroad man who had been a soldier, as I used to boast, "when he wasn't as big as Ed." That was a fact.

My father, Canadian born, had been brought from Chatham, Ontario, to Kansas City when he was only five or six. His forbears had founded Chatham; the family stock was German; eight generations back of me there had come to America one who spelled his name Greisler, a German Palatine. He was one of a group of Protestants who had left their homeland in the Rhine Valley, gone to the Netherlands, thence to England and embarked, finally, from Plymouth for New York. After the Civil War began, when my father was twelve, he ran away from home to Armourdale, Kansas, and enlisted in the Twelfth Kansas Regiment as a drummer boy. His father tried to get him out, but he drummed for the regiment until the end of the war. I used to listen to him tell

18

about the times when he went hungry or had to sleep in snow or rain with just a blanket. He was not injured by the hardships. I suppose there never was a man more healthy. In the twenty-seven years that he had that passenger run out of Ellis, I never knew him to lose a day. Nevertheless, what happened to him in the war was a visionary part of my young life. My brother Ed and I pumped out of him every scrap of what he could remember of his life as a drummer boy in the Civil War.

When the war was over and he was mustered out, he went to work in the railroad shops in the same town where he had enlisted, in Armourdale. Then he was put on the pay roll as a fireman, and after that was promoted to be a locomotive engineer. He was an engineer on the railroad until he retired. Of course, when he began, it was not the Union Pacific; what was being built westward out of Kansas City then was called the Kansas Pacific Railway. The train his engine hauled in that time supplied the construction gang that laid the first rails across the state. Great herds of bison sometimes blocked the right of way and were stampeded off only when the bulbous stack of his wood-burning engine threatened them with dragon snorts of smoke and fire. There were swarms of Indians, too, and they killed some of the men he knew.

Sometimes, but rarely, he would get a permit that let me ride with him up in the cab, from Ellis all the way to Brookville. At Fort Hays, only thirteen miles from where we lived, I'd see the blue-clad soldiers of the garrison and then, farther on, at Victoria, right beside the railroad station, I could see some graves of men my father said he knew.

"Indians killed 'em," he would say, and then, while his great monster shook and roared across the land, he would point out other places where whites and redskins had fought

19

and killed one another. On the run back, he always had the evening train out of Junction City. Waiting for that allowed us idle hours in which to see the sights at Brookville, but nothing gave me quite the thrill that came at nighttime, watching how he made that engine roar across the land.

At my father's nod the fireman would leap to sweaty action, swinging back the fire door with a devilish clang. In that moment of glare, each face in the cab turned as red as an Indian mask. With frantic grace the fireman would scoop coal from the tender, swinging the big shovel so expertly that the lumpy succession of black galaxies went in tight clusters to the center of the white-hot fire. Outside the engine cab the night would seem to moan and scream every time my father pulled the whistle cord. I watched the muscles writhe below the hair on his forearms when he used his hands to turn a cock or pull the throttle farther back upon its quadrant. I watched his face when he fixed his gleaming eyes in a gaze ahead into the headlight's yellow corridor through which we rode. The padded board on which I huddled bounced and throbbed and shook from side to side. Hot cinders bit me on the face.

If I seemed somewhat less than wide-awake I was allowed, a time or two, to yank the whistle cord myself or to let my hand ride with my father's big and greasy fingers as he pulled at the cotton rope that sent the bell into a brassy clamor. It was a perfect experience to ride in the midst of that fire-and-water miracle and to know that to the boss of it, my father, I was more important than his engine. The old engine was just our slave. Climbing down, at the end of the run, to the cinders of the right of way in Ellis, the part of me most tired would be my face, and it was tired from grinning in my hours of ecstasy.

The G. A. R. hall in Ellis was in the basement of the stone

schoolhouse. I got to know that place real well, because one year, when I was twelve, I guess, the Grand Army men decided to organize us kids into a drum corps, so we could march with them in their Memorial Day parade. Ten boys were chosen, and my father drilled and taught us all. We had to learn the way he learned to drum: one-twenty time at first, and later on we practiced the faster marching time. He bought me a snare drum that was good enough to take to war, and he taught me how to stand as soldiers do. The drilling of those days fixed on me, I suppose for life, the habit of putting my feet at right angles, heels together, with my hands at my side.

Chairs were placed close together around the walls of that G. A. R. hall, and every chair was squired by a big spittoon. There was a silken flag, fringed with stiff blue cords, a fine thing that stirred me every time I saw it uncased. There were stacks of muskets, with their bayonets fixed, in each corner of the room. There were rusty shell fragments, and on the walls big pictures of Lincoln, General Grant and others. The drum corps, the sound of drums, seemed to take me by the throat. I stamped around that hall behind my father until he fixed into my blood the rhythm of the beat for marching men. It seems as if I hear his voice and see the dust rise from the floor as he marked the time with his big foot and called out, "one step, one step, one step."

Most of the adult railroad workers of our town had been in the war. All the pain had leached out of their days of glory. They wore their uniforms on important occasions and gave one another military titles until there seemed to be no privates in the hall. They chewed tobacco, spat and yarned. What they all attempted in their yarning was to evoke the past, but my father had a skill that could really do this thing. With drumsticks and a drum, he could make them all sit straighter, make their eyes shine as they remembered.

On Decoration Day and the Fourth of July, when the G. A. R. marched, my father, with his drum, was up at the head of the parade and all us kids were there in back of him, and back of us were the fifers, making the shrillest kind of music. On such occasions I would tingle from the excitement of my own fancy until my skin was like goose flesh.

A drum did not satisfy my mother's notion of what constituted a proper musical education. My brother Ed had always been a successful rebel against such matters, but she had her way with me; I was sent once each week to Miss Cartwright for a piano lesson. As well as I remember, I was one of the three Ellis boys thus afflicted. There were seventeen round buttons arranged in a series of extraordinary curves over the promontories in the front of Miss Cartwright's basque. My attention would wander to those jet buttons when I could not keep it on the keys. I sometimes think that I would have been as much an insurrectionist against this culture as my brother Ed, except that one of the dozen Cartwright pupils was a girl named Della Forker.

I was a great marble player; in a time when marbles and spinning tops were the only games common to men of Ellis and the other towns along the railroad, I was the local champion. There were several of us boys who, practiced from the schoolyard games, had skill enough to hold our own and more in the big game. Where the men played was close to the stone buildings of the railroad, within the sound of its chattering telegraph instruments in the train dispatcher's office. A cinder surface there, hard packed by many feet to a smooth blackness, was the rendezvous of idling trainmen; engineers, conductors, firemen, brakemen and others gathered there before the start and at the end of all their runs. Occasionally, there was to be found in that assemblage some cowboy, a farmer, or even a soldier from Fort Hays. Scratched upon the ground we'd have a twenty-foot circle, and into the middle of this were massed twenty marbles from every player. Often there were a dozen of us playing, while other dozens watched us shoot.

Each player had his favorite shooting marble, of agate or onyx or glass; these were our taws, which we believed were fraught with what we had of luck. When your turn came to shoot, you'd take your taw and knuckle down on the edge of the ring. Any marble you knocked out of the ring you kept, and then took another shot. The trick was to keep yourself in position. I could make my taw obey me like a billiard ball. If you hit a marble squarely, your taw stayed at the point of contact, spinning away its momentum until it stopped. The men might play for money, but when kids played, the only prizes were those little plaster "keesters," which, in the big game, were always new and clean. That is why we liked to play with the men. They bought their marbles at the store, paying real money for them.

Us kids supplied ourselves with marbles by winning from the men. Neither Ed nor I ever saw the day, in our boyhood, when we dared spend good money for marbles. A German sense of thrift was our standard in such matters. We got that not from our father but from our mother. Although she was born in Rocheport, Missouri, her background, her feeling, her instincts were German. She spoke German to us when my father was not around; it was long since a strange tongue to him, but we children could understand and speak it with her. Now I have forgotten almost all my German, but this I do remember: In her tenderest moods my mother's words came boiling out of her in German.

While antique hunting on an autumn day in 1936 I went into a house near Saratoga where a sale of the contents was in progress. In a china closet there I saw some little flowered cards, and for a moment I almost felt as though I were twelve years old again. Those cards had all the power of a perfume to call up the past. It almost seemed to me that I could hear my mother exclaiming, in her German words, her deep pleasure over the exquisite calling cards I had provided for her.

In Ellis, except for staple goods, we did our shopping by mail. Every year we sent five cents in stamps to some Eastern house, so as to receive its catalogue. Another means by which we extended our knowledge of what was right and proper in the world outside of Ellis was by reading all the advertisements in the magazines we saw. We traded magazines around among the neighbors, but eventually my favorite, almost my Bible, was The Scientific American. However, I am not sure just where I saw the printed offer to set me up in business as an agent for these calling cards. Anyway, my mother, as she stirred, bare-armed, some creamy batter in a yellow mixing bowl, looked at me proudly and consented to be my first customer.

The calling card she selected, edged with scallops, was almost like a valentine. Against the white background of the stiff card was fixed a rich design of glossy, highly colored paper lace. Through a cluster of forget-me-nots, a cuff of lace and two loops of golden bracelet, was extended a likeness of a hand, patently that of a lady who had never cooked nor scrubbed. This hand clasped another that was just as white and lovely, and was chastely cuffed in lace obscured by leaves, two pinkish roses and a bud.

I had samples ready when the boom began. All Ellis ladies seemed to want such cards as Mrs. Chrysler had. I remember that there was a special good-luck card on which a warm and pinkish hand extended a gilded horseshoe wreathed with

red and yellow roses and a bluish ribbon on which was inscribed, "All joys be thine." The hand motif was much too
general, in my opinion. One of these hands held out a design
of lilies of the valley, white peonies and green leaves sur-
rounding an oak leaf on which were printed trembling letters
spelling, "To the one I love." The sample revealed that this
was intended to be a man's card. But what sort of man? His
like was not to be found among the railroaders in Ellis! Nor
was there any male customer for the gilt-edged card of baby
blue, with a turned-down pinkish corner. On that one the
sample name was "John B. Hard," hidden by a green-and-
brown bird's nest containing three greenish eggs. God alone
knows the meaning of that symbolism now, but certainly no
man of Ellis had the disposition to order any. Oh, beyond
a doubt that fad was addressed to women.

I was not trying to improve the tone of social life in Ellis.
I was trying to make a few nickels to spend for candy and
other things I wanted. Next my merchandising fancy was
caught by an advertisement of a house that offered induce-
ments to any who would solicit orders for its silverware.
What I displayed thereafter, from kitchen door to kitchen
door in Ellis, was a black case of imitation leather with nickel
clasps. When I unfastened these and raised the lid, I had
almost made my sale! The lid was lined with white satinette;
the box itself was lined with red plush which formed soft
slots in which were held three knives, three forks, three
spoons. Those women wanted silverware almost more than
they wanted food. In the course of five or six paydays, I sold
some of them four boxes, so that they had their silverware in
dozens. I had competition, though, and so my mother's offer,
plus her hairbrush, won me to another form of peddling. I
sold milk.

The words I commonly applied to those cows are not permitted to be shaped in type. For a while, milking, morning and night, was a chore I shared with Ed, but he was so much bigger that I had no choice but to do any job that he neglected; either that or take a beating. He hazed me pretty constantly, thereby driving me into a closer alliance with my mother. He was three years and three months older. There would have been another brother between us, but he died before I was born. The only other child in the Chrysler household was our little sister Irene. Consequently, when Ed got big enough to declare his independence of mother's hairbrush and all the cows, I became the one who had to milk the cows, to clean their stable, fork down hay and fodder or round them up when any wandered. But that was not all; I had to sell the milk and cream.

Every evening, as soon as the milking was over, I delivered milk from house to house. I carried a big open tin bucket full of milk and measured out each customer's share with a tin quart cup I carried with me. Wagon? I had no wagon, and if any customer wanted cream I had to make an extra trip. I delivered fifteen to twenty quarts or more each night. We had no ice at first; mother just had a little cellar, and in its cool dampness the milk, cream and butter, in ordinary weather, kept quite sweet.

Nobody paid for anything in Ellis until payday. I kept a record of my customers' obligations in a small account book carried in a hip pocket of my pants. On payday I collected at the rate of five cents a quart. For that I was rewarded. The cut that mother gave me was a cent on every quart.

Despite the taming influences of chores and money-making, I confess I raised my small share of hell. Maybe there is as much fighting among boys today; I can only say I do not think so. In the schoolyard we often had four or five fist fights in the fifteen minutes of recess. A kid who had a yellow streak would lead a dog's life; several that I knew ran away because they lacked the necessary toughness. If you could take your beating fighting back with all you had, you did not have to take so many beatings. We really had a tough environment there in Ellis. It was never any cause for wonder in me that Kansas took to prohibition early in its history. On railroad paydays the saloons were set like traps; likewise every few months when the cattle ranches paid their hands.

The saloons were placed as islands down the middle of a most informal street, a pathway really; and each saloon was surrounded by its hitching rack. When the cowboys' horses were standing in slant-hipped weariness, flank to flank around the saloon racks, that was a good time for timid folks to stay at home, indoors. But for us kids, the hoof clatter, the yipping and the shooting as a band of thirsty, paid-off cowboys rode into Ellis was prized above most of our local excitements. I have seen cowboys full of whisky and the devil pull their guns and throw a shot or two at some derby hat worn by a stranger at the station. I have seen them shoot out a few store fronts and ride their horses out of the mud and along the board sidewalks, but it was all in fun, and I never saw one less than perfectly polite to any woman. They seemed to have more respect for a woman than did any other sort of men. On occasions they did some killing, but I saw none of that. However, us kids used to pick up the pistol cartridges that would jounce loose from the belts of galloping cowboys when they rode in town on payday. I had a cigar box full. I never wanted to be a cowboy; that I can remember, thanks to what I had to do with cows at home, but I certainly aimed in those days to grow up tough.

Ellis grew civilized so fast, however, that barbarianism never had a valid claim on me. At first there was no paving whatever; when you stepped off the boardwalk, you were in the mud. Then a bank was organized, and we had a butcher shop where beef was sold. The butcher would give you liver for the asking. First thing we knew, there was a coalyard and a lumberyard. Somebody opened a rival of the first general store, and finally we had a regular post office apart from any store. The streets intruded farther and farther into the prairie. It was about 1889, when I was past fourteen, that my father built a bigger house with two stories. It had a shingled roof, a nice porch, and just above it a dormer window. Around the yard was a wooden picket fence; there were lilac bushes in the corner of the lot and some maples my father planted eventually were big enough to shade our yard.

There was no plumbing in Ellis that anyone could brag about, and it was an event when my father, a progressive citizen, bought a windmill so we could have running water. The next thing was a bathtub, for which he built a special room against the kitchen. He made it himself, by lining a wooden box with sheets of copper, shaping the metal with a steep slope at each end, enclosing this contrivance in a sheath of tongued and grooved boards. When it was painted we had something of which all the neighbors envied us. Until then, our baths were taken in a wooden tub out in the kitchen. At the rear of our yard there was a stable—we had four horses as well as three cows—and a coal shed. It seems to me that the back door of our house was the only one I ever used. The alley was a thoroughfare that led to temporary freedom from the chores I hated. If Ed or I ran away after dark to play with the kids, when we came home we always got a licking, because my mother was unfailingly strict. It was her law that we must not be out after dark. Sometimes we would hop the evening train, riding on the blind baggage thirteen miles to Hays. You could bet, as you approached the house through the back yard, that she would be sitting in the kitchen waiting with that hairbrush, and a hand that would hold you by the neck with a grip like iron. Still, on certain nights, the excitement was worth the fee.

Arranged along the alleys in the proportion of one to every house were rows of small structures that an anthropologist, if a stranger in the land, might have supposed were shrines. If they were shrines, then we were vandals, because on Halloween we used to discommode the town by roving all the alleys, tipping over every little house we found unguarded. Surely those pranks disqualified any member of our gang from ever being accepted as a hero of the Horatio Alger pattern. My sole excuse for such behavior is that when we came home on Sundays from the Methodist Church, my mother always said, "Take off those clothes." Probably, with the clothes I stripped off something of the spirit.

Since my mother made practically all the clothes we wore, this was her right; she knitted our socks, she made our shirts and made my sister's dresses, and when I was big enough to assert a need to have my legs incased in long pants, she took an old pair of my father's, opened up the seams, turned them upside down when she cut them to my measure, and then, wrong side out, made me a pair that I was proud to wear. Oh, she had a lot to do to keep us clad and fed. We ate enormously, like famished demons. All day Saturday she baked, and so, for help, she required that whole day out of Ed's life and mine. Of course, when I got into high school, Ed had been emancipated from home into a job.

My brother Ed, as husky as anyone that Kansas ever grew, always was aggressive. He was a boy who managed to make more money than a lot of Ellis men. But he surrendered some of his money-making chances to become an apprentice in the machine shops of the Union Pacific there in Ellis. Ed was going to learn a trade.

29

Certainly, in our town it was thoroughly accepted that a sound way to keep a boy out of mischief was to require him to use up some of his energy in work. It was the same with horses; when they were not worked, they bucked and kicked and made a lot of trouble. Even so, us kids had fun. My father gave me my first gun when I was fourteen, and at the railroad shops they cut it down to fit me. I was a good shot. Of course, I always loaded my own shells; we all did. Later on, for a Christmas present, my father gave me a dozen brass shells. He was quite liberal with us kids, but he was never so foolish as to suppose that it would be a kindness to permit his sons to loaf while their parents worked from dark to dark. I was in high school when Ed was an apprentice, but when the summer vacation began I got a job myself.

A fellow named George Henderson who had a grocery store had to keep his wife behind the counter while he pushed a two-wheeled cart around, delivering orders. I offered myself as a delivery boy and was hired at ten dollars a month. I went to work at six o'clock in the morning and was through by 10:30 at night. That store was long and narrow, with just a plain board counter. Practically all the stock was kept in wooden boxes and barrels. We used the scales to measure almost everything we sold; even smoking tobacco was measured out by the pound.

The next year, when I had finished high school, I went back into the grocery store to work for Henderson. He was paying me fourteen dollars a month, but I did not like those hours and I was not satisfied with either my money or my prospects. I wanted to quit the grocery store and learn about machinery. That made Ed sore.

"Why don't you be a boilermaker?" he would roar. "One machinist in a family is enough."

"I don't want to be a boilermaker," I'd yell back to him.

My father wanted me to go farther in school. One of the prosperous merchants of the town planned to send his son to Quincy College at Quincy, Illinois. He talked my father into a frame of mind to send me, too, so that his boy would not get homesick. I did not like the thought of college and I liked that other boy even less. I argued my case at home. Indeed, I nagged my father until at last he said:

"You can't learn machinery, and that's all I got to say. You cannot get to be an apprentice until I say the word, and I won't recommend you." That made me mad.

I went down to the shops and succeeded in being hired as a sweeper. The flooring there was made of fourteen-inch planks two and a half inches thick, splintery and slick with grease. I swept them as I think they never had been swept before. I had a stubborn streak in me. Some of the other dirty work a sweeper had to do was in connection with the cleaning of the engine-boiler flues. In Kansas, these pipes, or tubes, of rolled iron would become thickly caked with alkali. Each was about fourteen or sixteen feet long and weighed perhaps 150 pounds, thickened as they were with that stonelike deposit of alkali. I had to lug them on my shoulder seven or eight hundred feet to a timber shed. They were rolled around in there until they were clean; then the ends were cut off and new ends welded on. I carried miles, I guess, of boiler pipe, and swept the floor and did all the other kinds of work that fall to the lot of a janitor.

But I loved it; I loved to see the engines with their mysteries exposed. I envied the mechanics who understood their inner workings. I liked to handle tools. Even as a janitor I was allowed to sharpen, on the big power grindstone, any tool I brought from home, but then, almost any man in Ellis was permitted to do that. Why, once, while I was near the grindstone, an Indian came and sharpened his hunting knife.

31

I worked ten hours a day, and for that the railroad paid me one dollar.

After six months, I braced the master mechanic himself and asked his help. His name was Edgar Esterbrook, and afterward my brother Ed married his daughter.

"You want to be an apprentice, hey?"

"Yes, sir."

"Well, Walt, if ever anybody had a right to ask for the chance, it's you. You've stuck to your job and haven't belly-ached. The men like you. I'll tell you what I'll do. I'll speak to your father. That is, if you are sure you want to be a machinist."

"Yes, sir, I do." I was a cocky youngster and full of confidence, but I was shivering in my eagerness.

Mr. Esterbrook won my father over. So I began my four-year term as a machine-shop apprentice. My pay at first was five cents an hour. Who could ask a better chance?

· II ·

AMBITIONS OF AN APPRENTICE

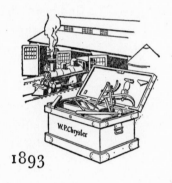

1893

"Tools Were What I Wanted"

· II ·

AMBITIONS OF AN
APPRENTICE

A TALISMAN that belonged to my father for more than
half a century became a treasured memento in my office; it was his steam gauge. To a locomotive engineer, a
steam gauge is as vital as his watch. On this cherished disk of
silver-gleaming metal, with a glass cover on its dial that my
two hands will barely hide, my father's life depended; oh,
and many other lives. So he had it tested often and guarded
it throughout his days. After he died my sister Irene, out
West, found it among some things he left, and sent it on to
me. This old steam gauge was my father's dearest implement,
but now for me it has become a sort of crystal ball.

Gazing upon its face, obliged no longer now to register
demonic pressures, it sometimes seems to me as if I can hear
my father's engine whistle blowing faintly to me on the wind
from far out of Ellis on the Kansas prairie horizon. What I
hear, of course, is just a shrillness in the traffic noises rising
from the street; yet it works a miracle! I can almost see the
bustling at the little Ellis station platform at the moment his
engine pulled the night train from Junction City into Ellis.
It was his engine; his in a way that a trooper's horse is his,
an extension of his power and intelligence, to defend, to
brag about and love. Sometimes the vision takes another

35

form and the engine, venting cautious chuff, chuff, chuffs, is nosing through a roundhouse door and I am down below the level of its wheels, working in a roundhouse pit with a sooty face and my arms grease-blackened, all my muscles hard and lean and young. Many times I have wished I really could hear again my father's engine whistle as I used to hear it just before it reached the Big Creek bridge. Well, music works a trick for my memory, too; a band marching up Fifth Avenue may send a bit of melody, just a bar or two, that touches things within my mind. It sets me thinking of a time when I was a machine-trade apprentice in the railroad shops, when I played a tuba in the band, played second base on the baseball team and walked, on Sunday afternoons, with Della Forker to the Big Creek bridge.

A Union Pacific shop apprentice! You can bet that I was proud. Just as every locomotive on the road flaunted a pair of antlers on her boiler shield beneath her headlight, so I should have had a badge to show that I was a cadet of that vast loom for weaving the Western half of the continent into the nation. Not merely the U. P. but railroading, the entire art as we then knew it, held my imagination in focus.

My opinion of myself had expanded tenfold when I became an apprentice. Everybody in Ellis knew that any apprentice had been required to pass an examination—a stiff one. Some boys failed to make the grade, but I had done so readily, because algebra was one of my good subjects. I had used algebra when I worked in the grocery store, to help George Henderson figure out his costs. I had used it, too, when we were building a house, but I had never used it to better effect on my life than when I worked out some of the examination problems that had to do with locomotive wheels and driving rods.

Tools were what I wanted as soon as my term began. Times

have changed a lot since then; nowadays an industrial company expects to furnish workmen with all their tools, but in my youthful days the unfailing sign of a skilled workman was the chest of tools he brought to any job. With good reason, he prized them above anything he owned. A good workman was likely to mistrust any tool whose metal had not been tempered by himself. But I had an even better reason for making mine: I lacked the money with which to buy them.

Years after I ceased to need them to earn a living those tools I made were brought from the attic of the old home in Ellis and placed on display in a glass case on the observatory floor, seventy-one stories up in the tower of the Chrysler Building. There, on a clear day, a visitor may look to a horizon nearly forty miles away, and by strolling around a corridor see in one quick panorama hundreds of densely populated square miles of this great land. Yet I am sure that one who neglects the view to gaze, with understanding, into that chest of tools I made, will have learned more about America than one who looks from an observatory window down into the uneven mass of steel, stone and brick that forms the city.

When I began to work at my trade, tools were crude, so that is probably why I see that mainly we owe the tremendous advances of the physical aspects of our civilization to new and better tools. Electric lights are a tool; the telephone is a tool; so is the motion picture, the radio and the automobile, to mention just a few. How can anyone be so shortsighted as to suppose that opportunities now are fewer? In a world that offers not only new and wonderful tools but likewise astonishing new materials, each of which is a fresh challenge to everything that men have made before, new human needs and bigger human problems are being revealed faster than a single human mind can even count them.

The first tool I made was a little pair of calipers; spread to

37

their limit, they could measure a diameter of four inches. They were copied from a pair belonging to another fellow in the shop. I made other things as need of them arose. One of the mechanics allowed me to look through a catalogue he had received from a big tool firm in the East. In there was a picture and a description of a depth gauge.

I had never heard of such a thing; there were none in the shop. When we had to measure the depth of a hole in a piece of metal, we explored the hole with a wire, marked it with a fingernail and then applied the wire to a ruler. Maybe such a measurement would be right to a sixteenth of an inch; nowadays we work in ten-thousandths of an inch.

Well, I got permission to keep that catalogue awhile, and made a depth gauge for myself. It was crude, but it was a great improvement over the wire, fingernail and ruler method. Fixed in a small stand was an arm, forked at the end; attached to that by a thumbscrew was a stem marked in divisions of thirty-seconds of an inch.

Thereafter in making a plug for a hole, I could make it right the first time, without a lot of needless filing and chipping. In a few months I made an even better depth gauge. Superior tools got me better chances in the shop. You see, I was ambitious to do all the kinds of work at which I saw the older men engaged. Consequently, I set to work to make myself a pair of granddaddy calipers, with legs almost as long as my arm. When I had those, I also had the nerve to ask to be allowed to help on the first lathe, the big one on which locomotive piston rods were turned.

Ankle-deep in oak shavings in the carpenter shop, I sometimes talked with and listened to an old carpenter. He chewed tobacco with such vigor that his blond walrus mustache was constantly in motion. Now and again he became motionless, tilted back his head as if to unmask a battery concealed in that brush of whisker hair, and fired a charge of brown juice at whatever target he had fixed his eyes upon. One day when I complained to him, for about the hundredth time, of night-shift men who borrowed tools and never brought them back, he pulled a sack aside and showed me an unfinished chest of just the proper size for tools.

"It's for you," he said. It took him several months to find enough time to complete that box to his satisfaction and mine, but meanwhile I had been etching my initials on all my tools.

I had read in The Scientific American how you could do that; first putting asphalt paint on the surface to be marked, then cutting out the desired pattern and finally applying acid. I sent ten cents to the magazine for a little bottle of asphalt paint and almost from the day it came all my tools were branded "W. P. C." in acid.

The Ellis band could turn a dull day into a time of rich excitement any time it marched and played. I was a part of that excitement. Even before getting out of high school they had used me in this organization of railroad employees to play the snare drum, and my friend, Charlie Keagy, played the bass drum. Thanks to my father's drilling and my membership in the drum corps, I had become a good drummer, but all the time I drummed I knew there were sweeter instruments. Hell, you could not serenade a girl with a drum!

My big brother Ed played a tuba in the band, and Joe McMahon played a slide trombone. We three slept in the same attic room at home; Joe was boarding with us, because his Irish father, a section foreman, who had become road master, had retired and moved the nice McMahon family to Kansas City, and Joe wanted to stay on in Ellis to serve out the final year of his apprenticeship in the machinist trade.

Almost every night we three had a pillow fight that did not

end until I, the smallest, was so mad that I was chasing them with a baseball bat. They teased me at home, they teased me in the shop and they teased me at band practice. In all the small towns I knew, band practice was first of all a device for fun; it gave an excuse for getting out at night, and hence a chance to meet the other boys and girls of other parents just as strict as yours.

When our band marched and played in Ellis, any young horses that happened to be among those hitched to the racks in town would pitch and rear, no matter how well our music had been rehearsed. But the thrill was compounded of much more than that; in front of all the stores, with false fronts instead of second stories, wooden awnings slanted out over the wooden sidewalks, supported as a kind of arcade on wooden posts; when half the town was lined up there to see and hear us, it was swell to be a member of the band.

Our uniforms were simply overalls and caps with long bills, so that when we marched, with red bandannas around our necks, we looked like locomotive engineers. The leader of the band was an engineer, Ed Pearson. He played a cornet. Well, I could read music, because I had taken piano lessons from Miss Cartwright when Della Forker did; moreover, I had practiced on our organ at home until I could play that too. But you can't play an organ with a marching band, and as I was tired of just beating a drum, I bought myself a B-flat clarinet. I tootled and tweetled on that instrument night after night until my mouth was sore.

One year, in our overalls and wearing big sunflowers, we band fellows rode, on railroad passes, to Kansas City and marched in the Priests of Pallas parade, an annual festival; Creole Belles, it seems to me, was what we played best that year. I think it was the next year when Ed, having more important engagements for his evenings, abandoned band practice and permitted his brass tuba to turn a greenish color from neglect. Ed was going with the daughter of Edgar Ester- brook, the division master mechanic; afterward, Ed and Mae were married. It was I who took Ed's place as tuba player. It made a big noise, and I liked it. I sent money to Kansas City and received a silver-plated tuba with a bell that had a gold burnish—a noble instrument. It was supported by a strap that went around my shoulder. You could play a solo on the tuba, but you were likely to be the only one who cared for it. Whenever I made mine grunt in practice or in earnest, I was having fun. Band or no band, however, I worked in the shop not less than sixty hours every week.

There was always a lot of horseplay around the shop when no boss was looking, and at times they might look in vain and not discover where the horseplay was; we had a hiding place. In the back side of one of the greasy pits the planking was incomplete, and through that empty blackness we could pass, with just a bit of squeezing, into a cozy little cavern big enough for four or five young fellows. The hideout had been formed as stealthily as if we who used it had been prisoners bent on escape. Well, whenever boredom came, escape was what we wanted.

In Ellis, playing cards was frowned upon by the Method- ists, and that was the religious group to which I belonged. Association with bad women, the use of whiskey, cigarettes or cards were as evil brands; if you wore any one of these brands, the respectable mothers of the town would see that you were kept far from all decent daughters. A lot of years have passed and I can take the chance involved by my confessing: in that hideout we played cards, we smoked cigarettes and on a few occasions we had a little beer. All these iniquities were prac- ticed in the earth below the shop floor, in the light of a candle stuck in a bottle's neck. Oh, how tough we felt ourselves to be!

That was fun, but it was not half so thrilling as the work I did when we overhauled an engine. Not books but the things themselves were teaching me what I wished to know. Wished? That word is not strong enough to describe my passion to learn about machines and the power that made them run. Concerning all the unfolding forms of magic which were then beginning to transform the continent, I was mad with curiosity.

As there were none in Ellis well enough informed to answer all my questions, I addressed myself in almost every mail to an Eastern oracle, The Scientific American. In that editorial office, whoever received the questions from subscribers must have thought that Walter P. Chrysler was the pen name of a dozen youths, at least half of whom were crazy. Yet many of my questions were answered; if you were a reader of the issue of November 5, in 1892, you may have seen a little of all that seethed in my mind. In that issue this was published:

W. P. C. asks what the Harden hand grenades for extinguishing fires are made of. *A.—Hand grenades for extinguishing fires are made by filling thin spherical glass bottles with a solution of calcium chloride, sal ammoniac or borax.*

2. A good insulating material that I can mold out for insulating storage-battery plates? *A.—Use gutta percha.*

3. Are there any two acids mixed together that will cause an explosion? *A.—Yes.*

4. Will sulphuric acid set fire to wood? *A.—Sulphuric acid will char wood by extracting the elements of water.*

5. Will the spray from the storage batteries set fire to wood? *A.—We do not think it will set fire to wood.*

For a long time I had been accustomed to making things I wanted when I could not buy them. I had made my first pair of ice skates; later on I made a good shotgun; but in the shops I made, on my own time, a model locomotive.

What I made was a twenty-eight-inch model of the engine my father drove; that was the standard type, which had a four-wheel drive. We had no blueprints then, so I had to do it all myself, laying out my own proportions. Then I took a solid piece of iron and started in to drill and chip and file.

A sculptor trying to release in marble some shape of beauty that is captive in his mind can give no more loving care and craftsmanship to what he does than was done by me as I created that locomotive model. Of course, that engine had to live within my mind so real, so complete that it seemed to have three dimensions there. That, so it seems to me, is what the fault is when someone fails to learn from books. My fingers were like an intake valve through which my mental reservoir was being filled; of course, my eyes and ears were helping in the process, but what I learned with my fingers and my eyes together I seem never to forget.

When the engine model was complete and had many yards of track to run upon, I made it run all around our yard. When its tiny whistle blew, you should have seen my father's mustache widen with his grin of pride.

It must have been about the end of my second year that trouble came. At first I had been paid five cents an hour; for a ten-hour day I got just half of that dollar I had received when I was only a sweeper. But through my second year I got ten cents an hour, and at the time I speak of I was within a few weeks of being entitled to the third-year rate of pay, twelve and a half cents an hour. That was enough money then; I slept and ate at home, and my mother still made most of the clothes I wore. If I worked on the night shift, my mother packed an oblong dinner pail with food enough to fill me up. If I worked days, I went home to lunch—not lunch; that was dinner, then.

Midday, when the shop whistle blew and told Ellis women to get ready for their men, I rushed, with the other soot-and-grease-stained mechanics, to a trough where we washed up. When I had been a sweeper, to fill that long blackened trough with water about ten minutes before noon had been a chore of mine. When all of us had washed our faces, necks and hands in that trough, the water was a dirty fluid, gray and bubbly.

One day as we began working in the afternoon, the wash trough, neglected by the sweeper, still was filled with dirty water on which floated an iridescent scum. Some of the men were idling there as I resumed the filling of a journal box with grease and wool waste so as to pack this lubricant around the axle end. I was bending over a tub of this grease and wool waste when I got a slimy blow upon the face and ear. Oh, I was mad! A fellow named McGrath had a dripping hand when I looked up; he had, I knew at once, thrown that rag after slopping it in the dirty water in the trough.

I said—well, never mind what I said. The first thing I thought of was going after him. I grabbed deeply into the tub of wool waste and started for him; he ran through a big door, which he slammed behind him. I knew he would not loiter outside long, because he had to run in the direction of the office of the general foreman, Gus Neubert.

I stood before the door, poised as if to throw from second to home plate, and addressing myself over my shoulder to some who mocked my anger, I said, "I'll soak that so-and-so right in the mouth." Then the latch clicked softly, a hinge squeaked, and I flung first one handful and then the other. But it was not McGrath that I splattered in the face; it was Mr. Neubert. He fired me before he had the stuff wiped off.

For some days thereafter I felt as if I had been banished

from earth. I was sick; nothing in the world was half so important as my apprenticeship. Maybe my brother Ed helped out by speaking to Mr. Esterbrook, or it may have been my father. At any rate, the master mechanic sent for me. When I stood before his roll-topped desk piled up with papers, he gave me a lecture which I received contritely.

"That McGrath," I said, "he made me mad. I was working when ——"

A vast man, Mr. Esterbrook. When he chuckled, his watch chain, that barely stretched across his vest, moved up and down; I saw it moving then and knew just a trace of hope.

"Next time," he said, "you wait and see who is coming through the door, or catch McGrath outside on your own time. Now, if you apologize to Mr. Neubert, maybe he'll let you come back."

Well, then, with a hangdog manner, I went to Mr. Neubert. I begged his pardon while tears splashed on my chest. He beckoned me to follow him outside the shop where no others could hear him dress me down. For more than half an hour he told me things. At last he said: "This must be a lesson to you. If it ever happens again, I'll fire you sure! And you'll never come back."

When you see a retriever frisking in the ecstasy that comes when you get out your gun, you will know just how I felt when I went back to work. That fright did me a lot of good. From that time on I really settled down to learn, because I knew then just how much I loved mechanics. And now, in 1936, out in Kansas City, on our pay roll, there is the name of a gentleman, a friend of mine, now quite old — the name is Neubert.

One night the man that I was helping underneath a locomotive stopped his work to look around us cautiously. Where others like ourselves were working on locomotives laid up for repairs, the darkness of the shop was torn by the orange flames of coal-oil flares. Upon the gaunt stone walls and cobwebbed trusses of the ceiling gigantic engine shadows alternately swelled and shrank.

"I'm going uptown." His voice was low and meant for just my ear. I was his apprentice helper, and devoted to old Arthur Darling.

"You'd better not," I warned him, scared on his account. "They'll fire you sure if you get caught." Sometime before, Darling had come into Ellis and got a job in the shops. He had worked in many places, but last of all in the Santa Fe shops. In our Union Pacific shops what was regarded as his best skill was in setting engine valves. He surely was an expert, and Mr. Neubert had put me with him as his helper, so that I could learn to do a valve job too. Men who could were hard to get. The pulling power of a locomotive depends upon the proper setting of its valves. Why, even now I can lie in bed at night and tell, from the sound of a distant locomotive as it labors with a heavy train, whether its valves are rightly set; when they are, there is a smooth even cadence to the puff, puff, puff, puff as the engine works. For that knowledge, and unnumbered other things I know about machines and metal and men, I owe a great debt to that grease-blackened old mechanic, Darling. Really, I owe him more than I can measure. The way of teaching in that time, whereby the good craftsman passed on his knowledge to an apprentice in the most practical way of all—while he worked—to my way of thinking was a most effective system. Certainly after the lapse of many years I feel impelled to say that no apprentice ever had a better teacher than Arthur Darling was to me.

"You just go ahead with these valves," he instructed as he moved away out of the light we shared. "I'll be back around twelve o'clock," he said, and vanished.

46

I was scared on his account.

I had begun to feel a warm affection for him. Although he was inclined to be almost surly when others tried to learn out of his vast experience, with me he was quite different; he wanted me to share his understanding. Knowing him was almost like getting away from Ellis, because he knew so much of other roads and of strange locomotive species we had never overhauled. He was the first really to teach me how to handle steel; he had been better educated than the Ellis men in the shop, and was so sure of himself when engaged with mathematics as to make me marvel.

"Listen," he had cautioned me, "when you start a valve job always take your own port marks! No matter if someone says he has taken them already; you take your own port marks and you won't go wrong."

You can bet I did not want to see the last of such a friend. I did not want to see him fired. So that night when he went on a spree, I struggled with that mechanical enigma to save his job.

The wheels, axles, main connecting rods and valve gear had been connected. I knew I had a chance, at least, if I could complete the job before the general foreman came to work in the morning. The rocker arm was put in its middle position. Then the valve stem was adjusted until it was in the center of the valve face. I placed the crank on the forward center, and the full part of the forward-motion eccentric above and that of the backward-motion eccentric below the axle. To fasten them temporarily, I tightened up the set screws and threw the link down until the block came nearly opposite to the end of the eccentric rod. It gave me satisfaction when I realized this was a puzzle I could work!

I was so intent on solving it that it startled me when Darling crawled under there and stood beside me. It was midnight; he had come back to check me up.

He ticked off what I had done. There was another helper there, but he was younger and just a little dumb.

"You're all right, Walt." Darling slapped me on the back. "I'm going back uptown. Around three o'clock I'll be back and take a look."

"Come on," I pleaded. "Crawl up in the engine cab and take a sleep. First thing you know you'll get it in the neck. They'll fire you sure."

"Nope! Going uptown. But wait a minute. I'll run those wheels around."

Big cast-iron rollers were put in place against the driving wheels; then, with pinch bars and ratchets, we could tighten screws until the weight of the locomotive was entirely on the rollers. Then, by pulling on a pinch bar, a man could turn the drive wheel of a standing locomotive. The other helper and I pulled the pinch bars, and as we turned the wheels, Darling observed the travel of the valve and made sure that it was equal to the throw of the eccentric.

In a mumble he explained to me just what he was doing, and why. Then, with an endorsing wave of his hand, he walked out again. I proceeded with the job to its conclusion. In the months that followed I do not think he completed three valve-setting jobs. Because I could do his work and because I covered him up, he warmed to me, and my experience, in this field of valve setting, far exceeded that of many journeymen. Old Darling said that I was a great young mechanic, and it is important that in my heart I agreed with him.

Sure I was cocky! I thought I was quite a kid. Long before our trains were equipped with air brakes, I had made myself understand how this Westinghouse contrivance worked and how to put it on an engine; my information came from the Westinghouse Company.

For compressing air there was a steam-driven air pump on the locomotive, and a reservoir, either on the tender or the engine, in which the compressed air was kept under pressure. The tender and each car had a cylinder and piston and a triple valve underneath its body; the piston being connected to the brake levers. Each car had a pipe extending along its bottom, and this was connected to the brake cylinder. I understood it long before the Union Pacific determined to equip its trains with this improvement. Consequently, when we did get air brakes, I got the job of putting them on the division locomotives. That was in the last year of my apprenticeship, I was getting fifteen cents an hour, but I was getting extra for examining firemen who wanted to be promoted to be engineers. They had a car rigged up with all the air-brake equipment. As I would show a fireman how it worked, I'd be thinking to myself: "What the hell do I want to stay around here for? With what I know, I could get a job in China!"

The next thing to come along was steam heat for the trains. We chucked out the old-fashioned little coal stoves that were the cause of so many horrible fires in train wrecks. I had been writing letters East, to technical magazines and other sources, so that I knew how to install that equipment, too, and got the job. Then along came electric signals. By that time I was primed with sufficient understanding of electricity to do this job. Naturally, as fast as I learned a thing that was new around the Ellis shops, I had to show it off, but in showing off I gained a lot of experience. I had a sense of hurry. I'd think: "Gosh, here I am already twenty-two—and still in Ellis."

Della Forker and I were waltzing in the G. A. R. Hall on a Saturday night. Her olive-tinted young throat was soft in a wrapping of velvet; just at the level of my mouth was her dark hair that waved back from her forehead into a Psyche knot. We were engaged; we had music aplenty in our hearts, and it was no concern of ours what sort of squeaky tune the other couples heard. Of course, for an ordinary dance, our crowd could not afford to import a four-piece orchestra from Junction City; we took our music raw out of a piano thumped by a thin colored girl, and a violin that was squeezed and maltreated by a lanky fiddler. It was fine to be engaged, but how could we get married on $1.50 a day?

Mr. Forker, Della's father, was a leading merchant of the town. His hobby was fast harness horses; he used a sulky, and found satisfying triumphs in dusty races on the prairie as he coaxed some high-shouldered, lathered pacer to throw its hoofs ahead of all the other horses in a race. I could not ask the girl to leave her home on what I could provide when we were first engaged, and anyway, we were agreed that there were better chances almost any place outside of Ellis. If we were civic traitors to our women-ruled community, well, then all small towns are filled with youthful traitors. Besides, I fairly ached to get around, to work in other shops, to learn and to have adventures.

As for romance, I showed a wisdom far beyond my years when I obeyed the inner promptings that told me the world did not contain a girl to match my Della.

Lying on my desk there is a letter from an elderly man in our Kansas City branch, who wants to see me again, shake hands and have a talk, "the same," he writes, "as we had many years ago when you passed through Kansas City on your way home from Europe. I can feel your hand on my shoulder and see the sparkle in your eye." He has signed his letter, "your friend, Gus." My spirit, as his does, warms to old memories. In those days he was "Mr. Neubert."

Mr. Neubert had left his place as general foreman in our shops; he had left the Union Pacific to take a more important job with the Atchison, Topeka & Santa Fe.

Long before this he had completely forgiven me for that awful blunder when I socked him in the face with axle grease and wool waste. May be it was his going away from Ellis that made me so determined to leave when my apprenticeship was served. It was nearly at an end when they learned at home that I was in a desperate mood, that I was full of a crazy scheme to seek work in another town.

My father spoke to me in deadly earnest, warning me about the men he saw stealing rides on trains. "Maybe, Walt, when they began they thought they wanted to see more of the world, to learn more things. What's the use of going off to another railroad to look for a job? The best railroad in the world is the Union Pacific. On this road you've got a lot of friends and so have I. In another week or so you will be getting a journeyman's pay. Mr. Esterbrook tells me there isn't a better mechanic in the roundhouse or the shops than you. You should stay right here in Ellis; settle down."

Settle down? Why, that was just the trouble! I'd never had a chance to put myself in a situation from which I could settle down, or so I felt. You couldn't hell around in Ellis. If the gang even had a keg of beer out at the ball field, every mother knew it and spoke her mind.

Besides, I just knew that any other town was better than Ellis; any time I met a stranger, no matter where he came from, he knew things that were unknown in Ellis. To my parents, my defense was that I had ambition and wanted to get ahead.

I was too big to lick with the hairbrush, so my mother tried to win me to her way of thinking by crying; at intervals she pleaded with me to have some sense and listen to my father.

51

She would remind me that not all cooking was like that I got at home, and then she would shed more tears. I could not argue; what I did was to snatch my hat, rush out and slam the door. I did not want to hear their arguments, because what they had to say, I knew, was far from foolish. After all, they did like me at the shop.

I was a good worker. I always tried to please the man I worked for; even though I was a good mechanic, if I was asked to sweep the floor, I'd sweep it. However, I had my mind made up. I went to see the master mechanic, Mr. Esterbrook.

"You've been mighty nice to me," I blurted out as I walked up to his desk. "That I am a machinist is something I owe to you. I'll never forget it either."

"Why, Walt, I'm glad you've done so fine, I'll ——"

"But I'm going to quit, Mr. Esterbrook."

His face changed completely. The smile with which he had accepted my thanks faded like a light blown out. He was hurt and astonished.

"Is anything the matter, Walt?"

"No, sir. Not a thing. It's just that I want to get more experience. I think I'm a good mechanic—say, I know I am." I saw him grin, because of my habitual willingness to appraise my qualities at their proper value. "I can do any job you ask me to, Mr. Esterbrook, but I want to learn more things."

"Walt," he said solemnly, "you are a good mechanic; as good as any we've got. You mustn't quit."

"I'm sorry."

"Where are you going?"

"I'm going to try to get a job on the Santa Fe."

"Where at?"

"Arkansas City. Mr. Neubert will give me a job."

Some days before, I had written a letter to Mr. Neubert—

to my friend Gus, I mean to say—and he had written me that he would find a place for me. He did too. I got a long envelope from him; it contained a letter in which he told me to go to the Santa Fe shops at Wellington, Kansas. With it he enclosed a letter of introduction to a man named Sherwood.

My mother packed a basket full of food for me to eat on the long day-coach ride to Wellington. It was far to the southeast from Ellis; down in Sumner County on the border of the Indian Territory. I simply had to get away. I know that now. I had to give myself a chance to be a man away from home.

· III ·

JOURNEYS OF A ROUNDHOUSE MECHANIC

1897

"I Knew The Answer To My Lonesomeness"

· III ·

JOURNEYS OF A
ROUNDHOUSE MECHANIC

ONE time when Mrs. Chrysler and I went up to New London and saw the crews of Yale and Harvard race, a lot of my past was revealed; not to others, but to me. For just about half a minute I had the feeling of being a he Cinderella and getting a warning not to stay at the ball too late.

We had gone up there in our first big boat, a beautiful thing with perfect lines expressed in mahogany, white paint and gleaming brass. Then, after the races, we had gone for dinner and to dance at the Hotel Griswold; that's where everybody was that night, or so it seemed. At the top of the thickly carpeted stairs, just before we went down to the floor to dance, Mrs. Chrysler touched my arm.

"See that big white-haired man in the orchestra. Isn't that Joe McMahon?"

In all that pink-and-amber dimness, the first thing I looked for among the musicians was a slide trombone. When I found it, sure enough, the bulky, red-faced fellow blowing into it was Joe McMahon. Until the tune was finished, we stood there, and then: "Hi, Joe!"

"Hello, Walt; and, say, if it isn't Della!"

We three talked of Ellis, Kansas, where we all grew up, until Joe had to pick up his trombone again when the leader began tapping with his baton on his music stand to end the interlude; but after that for hours I was remembering fragments of a longer interlude when Joe and I were roving in the West; each of us a machinist; each accustomed to play in bands; each inured to freight-train traveling and the lack of money. Many and many a time I hopped a freight train when I wanted to go somewheres else in search of work. Does anyone suppose I don't know what it means to hunt for work?

There were some pictures on the walls and the room was bright. The golden-oak varnish of the roll-top desk was marred with nicks and scratches; its bottom drawer, nearest where I stood, had been scuffed by shoes until there was no varnish left on its face. This was the office of the boss, of the division master mechanic, in Wellington, Kansas, on the Santa Fe. He was seated in his swivel chair, there at the desk, reading the letter of introduction I had handed to him. His name was Sherwood; to me, his precise speech sounded peculiar, foreign; afterward I was to learn that Mr. Sherwood, no longer young, was an Englishman. He wore whiskers of a kind we used to classify as "curtains."

"Mr. Neubert says you are a good mechanic."

"That's right, I am." I knew Mr. Sherwood took his orders from Mr. Neubert.

"You appear pretty young to be an experienced journeyman mechanic. How old are you?"

A switch engine passed along the yard tracks outside the window just then, its bell making a great clamor. My eyes were on the engine as I answered, "Twenty-three." Actually I was ten months younger.

"Twenty-three does not suggest that you have had much experience," protested Mr. Sherwood doubtfully. "Can you set valves?"

"Yes, I can do a valve job—good enough for Mr. Neubert."

58

Mr. Sherwood's eyes roved over me as if he were still unconvinced.

"Can you lay out shoes and wedges?" That is another accurate and difficult job connected with the repair and overhauling of locomotives.

"Yes, I can lay out shoes."

"You look too young to be so experienced. Why, I've got older men than you around these shops to whom I would not intrust such important and difficult jobs. But on the strength of Mr. Neubert's recommendation, I'm going to put you to work. We have three rates of pay for journeyman mechanics: Twenty-seven and a half cents an hour for the best ones; twenty-five cents an hour for the next best, and twenty-two and a half cents an hour for the less-experienced fellows— lathe hands who come here to Wellington because they want to learn some more about their trade."

"I'm not just a lathe hand. I'm an all-'round shop man."

"We shall see. You'll have to work two weeks before we say what rate of pay you get."

"All right. I'll work two weeks. But if I don't get the top pay I don't want the job."

"A cheeky young fellow." Mr. Sherwood looked for confirmation of this verdict in the eyes of an assistant who sat near him.

"No," I declared. "I'm just a good mechanic."

Mr. Sherwood passed a hand across his mustache, and I think he wiped off a smile; at any rate, he instructed me to report to the general foreman, Hart—Bill Hart. As we said in those days, my dander had "riz"; all those questions as to my ability were wounds that went deeply into my pride. At home everybody knew I was a really good mechanic. Of course, in the Ellis shops we had not been equipped to do certain heavy work with frames and boilers, but I had proved

59

my capacity to do the really complicated jobs. Probably I knew it just a little too well that day, because I think my manner rubbed Hart, the general foreman, the wrong way.

"You can set valves, hey? Well, there's a job." He indicated with his thumb a locomotive, one of a new type lately purchased by the Santa Fe. Concerning it, of course, I was entirely green. But I went to work, starting in to take my port marks. In a little while, Hart hurried toward me, waving a greasy hand impatiently as if to flag me.

"No, no, you don't need to take those port marks all over. I took them yesterday."

Deliberately, I took another steam-chest cover off before I answered. I did not want to be abrupt. But when I spoke, the best that I could do was to say, "Maybe so, Mr. Hart, but if you want me to set these valves, then I'll take my own port marks." I was not going to forget so soon in my journeyman career the advice old Arthur Darling had given me. Whatever he said to me had sunk in.

Hart glared at me. Now, as I think back on it, I don't blame him. My manner must have been irritating to a man with a general foreman's responsibility. However, one of the helpers who stood by spoke to me out of the corner of his mouth as Hart, after bawling me out, strode away.

"He couldn't set these valves himself," the youngster said. "He tried yesterday, and now you've been put on the job just to show you up. He's trying to rawhide you."

"Yeah?" I went all over that engine then. In the cab I discovered a few things that were new to me, but when I looked at the reverse lever, I saw that a plug was missing from the quadrant slot, a plug designed to prevent the lever from being opened too wide. I put a plug into that hole and grinned to myself as I left the cab. Then I took the valves out, looked at them and put them back. I knew they were all right. In a space of time much shorter than is usual on a valve job, I had the drive wheels off the rollers. Then I went to Hart and told him I was ready for another job.

"What?" He roared this query.

"She's ready."

"Chrysler, you mean to tell me those valves are set in this short time?"

"Yes. Take her out. She's all right."

"And you told me you were a valve man! Well ——"

"Sure I'm a valve man. I tell you that engine ——"

"Chrysler, if that engine does not pull the way she should when she's fired up—well, you won't have a job."

"Hook her to a string of cars; she'll take 'em away. What else you got for me to do?"

They fired the engine up at once and she pulled just like I had said she would. Sherwood sent for me a little while later and asked about that engine. I had refused to reveal anything to Hart, but to the master mechanic I explained about the plug. He chuckled, and thereafter I was put to work on air brakes. I got the top rate of pay, but, unhappily, I continued for a while to be too cocky.

Wellington was so much bigger than Ellis that I felt myself to be a regular city guy. I found things new and exciting. However, the thrill of a young fellow making his living away from home for the first time soon waned and the taste of freedom began to pall on me. First thing I knew I was as lonesome as a fellow could be; what I suffered from was homesickness. I did not have any friends, I hated living in the hotel, I hated the two-mile walk to work, and I hated eating my dinner out of a bucket. Back in Ellis, the only time I had ever carried a dinner pail was when I worked on the night shift; days I had always gone home at noon and stuffed myself until I was full of one of my mother's

wonderful dinners—lunch they call them now. She would
have been scornful if she could have seen the wedge of
soggy apple pie that the hotel waitress had dropped in my
bucket on top of a couple of juiceless sandwiches. I sat there
wishing I had brought my tuba, so I could join a band in
Wellington; then I was glad I hadn't and simply sat and
wished that I was home and hadn't been so foolish as to
squander all my money more than a week before pay day.

I sat outside the roundhouse on a railroad tie, my elbows
on my knees and my hands hanging between them limply.
Then, directly under my eyes, I became aware of an enormous pair of feet. I knew who they belonged to, a fellow
named Prince, a boilermaker, the biggest fellow in the shops.
Seems to me he must have stood six feet three or four; the
top of my head came just about to the level of his mouth.

"Don't you want a cigarette, Chrysler?"

That boilermaker had a tender heart. Of course, I wanted
a cigarette. He handed me the makings and I rolled one in
a fretful hurry.

As I felt the first drag go deep into my lungs, and breathed
it out, I began to grin, and twisted my head so I could look
up into the face of this good-natured giant.

"You wanted that one bad," he said. "How's it happen
you lack cigarettes?"

"Broke," I said.

"Get a sack of makings," he advised.

"That's what I smoke," I said, "but till pay day comes I
won't even have a nickel."

I grinned and Prince grinned back with a warmth and
understanding. I had been too proud to bum a cigarette,
but when he came and offered one, that boilermaker made
a friend. Thereafter in Wellington, Prince and I were pals,
chasing around together. Of course, that made me feel a

whole lot better, having a companion for my idle hours, but I continued to hate the drab uninviting hotel food.

One day at the shop, as I complained to a sympathetic old fellow, a blacksmith, he said, "Say, I've got a vacant room up at my house. If you want to move your things in and live with us, why, my wife and I would love to have you."

They were the finest, most-devoted couple anybody ever saw. All he charged me for my room and board was twelve dollars a month and, my, his wife really could cook! I began to be almost happy. Of course, it was not as good food as I got at home, but after the hotel, it seemed to me that not only my meals but the whole world had a better taste. Of course, that big fellow, Prince had much to do with how I felt. The laughs we had together!

But even through my homesick spell I continued confident. I was getting all the best jobs to do around the shop, and I knew my skill in fixing locomotives was a cause of satisfaction to the bosses. Possibly, that upset my sense of values, but I think an even bigger factor was that I had not then replaced the discipline of home with self-discipline. Lacking that, any human being soon finds trouble.

A circus had arrived in Wellington; not a big one, but still a circus. There was going to be a free parade, and I wanted to see it; so did a dozen others in the shop. They chose me as spokesman, and I walked up to Bill Hart, wiping my hands on a piece of waste. We wanted, I explained to him, to get off long enough to see the parade.

Hart folded his arms and stared at me. Each half of his big mustache seemed to move independently. In about two seconds he was in a rage.

"Are you crazy? What's the matter with you fellows? No! No! No!"

In his quite proper loss of patience, Hart raved. What

the others did not hear him say they could interpret from his half-frantic gestures. So, when I went back to report, they all got sore. Our dignity, which, I have discovered, is a lot more important than almost any other human factor, had been wounded. We'd show Hart, we would.

We washed up, took off our overalls and tramped uptown. Oh, that was a poor parade. Maybe they had elephants and clowns and a Queen of Sheba; I don't remember though; all I can recall is that I stood on the curbstone wishing I had been less of a fool. I began to see that it was more than Bill Hart that I had deserted. I had left the railroad. Suppose all the other men of the Atchison, Topeka & Santa Fe Railway were to take a simultaneous notion to go off the job and watch a circus. I remember how wilted, how tawdry the band musicians looked in their wrinkled uniforms, and I found no music in the sounds they were expelling from their brass horns. In about two hours we were back, and I had no more than hooked up the bib of my overalls than I saw old Sherwood striding toward me. If he had been the blustering kind, I would have blustered back, I guess, but he did nothing of the sort. He was exceedingly solemn, quiet.

"In years of railroad experience," he began, "nothing like this has ever happened to me. You ought to be fired. Every one of you ought to be fired here and now. You know that. I know it. So, it seems to me I'll do no good by doing something that I can do. You know I can do it?"

"Yes, sir."

"Well," he said, "I'm not going to fire any of you. I am simply going to hope that never so long as you call yourselves railroad men will any of you do a thing like this again."

I was just about ready to cry, myself, and I think the

others felt as I did. We knew we had behaved quite badly.

"I'm sorry, Mr. Sherwood. I wish I had not been so foolish. Mr. Hart, we thought, made it a little tough for us boys in the way he said we could not go. I'm awfully sorry and I feel that all the other boys are sorry. I promise you I'll never do anything like this again."

Mr. Sherwood shook his head from side to side and walked away. He had all the best of that argument without saying another word.

My mother kept on wanting me at home; so did my father. In his letters he would point out the advantages I would have if I came back to work in the Ellis shops of the Union Pacific; mother simply let me see that she was unhappy. But she was not alone in that; I had liked my freedom, but I had not liked being sure of clean clothes only when I carried them to a wash woman myself; some of the time I had not liked the food I got; at home my mother always cooked things she knew her younger son would relish. I missed my parents, I missed my home and I missed Della Forker. We corresponded faithfully. To clinch the matter, I got a letter from Frank Merrill, who was then master mechanic. He offered me a job at thirty cents an hour—three cents above the best rate for journeymen in the Ellis shops. So I quit the Santa Fe and, riding on a pass that came as soon as I accepted Merrill's offer went home to the finest meal any prodigal ever ate.

The new job was that of night mechanic—that is, I was the head man at night. I was the one at the roundhouse to whom the dispatcher's office telephoned when they wanted an engine for a certain train; when I got such a call, it was my responsibility to see that the boy called the engine crew and that the hostler put fire in the boiler, got up steam, took her across the turntable and down to the water tank, that he had her entirely ready to take a passenger train. Likewise it was my responsibility to see that the engine that had pulled the train into Ellis was properly treated when the hostler brought her into the roundhouse. There was a book in the roundhouse, a sort of work journal in which each engineer, as he finished a run, would report the kind of repairs needed by his engine—the boiler to be washed, flues to be calked, air brakes to be adjusted. That was one thing about my father: he knew so well how to handle a heavy train that his engine only rarely needed more than the minimum attention. Often he just wrote on the book: "Oil the trucks and driving boxes." Some of the men used to call him "Oil-the-trucks Hank."

Restlessness began to afflict me when I had been home only a few months; after Wellington, of course, Ellis seemed smaller than it had before I went away. But whenever I complained, my mother cried softly into her apron, for she knew what this portended. It seemed to me that I could not make anyone understand except Della Forker. I could tell her that I was ambitious and she would nod; it seems to me, I even dared to tell her that I intended, some day, to be a master mechanic. Of course, I realized I had to learn a lot before I could really hope to have that dream fulfilled, and that was why I wanted to go to a bigger place—so I could get more experience. Most of the time, even in my own mind, I was pretty vague about what I was going to do. But finally I put in a request for a pass to Denver and quit my job again.

I took a little suitcase with me, some calipers and a ruler wrapped inside my overalls; also I had the lunch my mother had put up for me in a shoe box, and there was a third piece of baggage. In a clumsy bulbous imitation-leather case I had my silver tuba with its golden burnished bell. This trip

I was prepared to avoid all moping. Through the night of that twelve-hour day-coach journey I used the tuba for a pillow.

In Denver I got a job in the shops of the Colorado & Southern. I did not like the place; it was wild and reckless. Along almost any street where I wandered of an evening fierce-looking, dissipated men would panhandle you for a nickel or a dime. They might whine with their lips, but with their eyes they were demanding. All the evil things feared by my father and my mother seemed likely to be coming true in Denver. I worked two weeks and quit.

Cheyenne, Wyoming, was where I headed for next. No pass this time. I met a conductor of the Union Pacific, and explained that I was Hank Chrysler's son.

"I can't deadhead you, kid. I'm sorry. Can't tell who might see me."

"No, listen. Not me; just the tuba. Leave it at the round-house in Cheyenne."

"All right. Give me the suitcase, too, if you want."

That made it easy. I just strolled down the yards to where a switch engine was kicking the last cars into a freight train; some of the cars were empties, and finally I came to one the door of which gaped six or seven inches. That meant there were men aboard. I pushed it wider, looked quickly up and down the tracks and then scrambled inside. There were half a dozen frowsy whiskered men curled up on the floor in there. One snarled at me, "Fix that door the way you found it." I fixed it quickly and settled down, my back against the freight car's wall. Well, that's the way I started.

I have forgotten much of Cheyenne, of Laramie and Rawlins; I worked in those places and a lot of others. Some-times when I could manage, I joined the local band. They had a good band in Laramie; as I recall it, it was there that

I found Joe McMahon, and we knocked around a while, parted and then got together again down in Salt Lake City.

There is no order in my recollection of those times. I found jobs in many places, yet I never seemed to find the job I hunted. Often I was broke, but if I went hungry, that was simply due to bad management. The important thing is that I never have forgotten how it feels to rove around this country hunting work. A few years ago I put up some money for an expedition to fetch live animal specimens from Africa, but I sometimes think I'd like to send another expedition through the West to see if it could find on some old branch-line water tank the initials W. P. C. with an arrow through them to show any following friend the direction I had gone.

The tuba was better than a passport in any town that had a band. The first band-practice night I would get acquainted with all the young folks of the town. I was a pretty good dancer and I danced plenty. At the same time, in the shops I was learning more and more; I learned something from every good mechanic with whom I worked; I learned the workings of a variety of engines; I learned shop practices; but most important, I learned a lot about men, and still more about Walter Chrysler.

I lacked patience then; I wasn't willing to stick around a shop to prove that I was good. If they did not appreciate me, if any foreman dressed me down, I'd get my time, pack up my bag, forward my tuba and head for the next shop town. Of course, I was spending money as fast as I made it. Spending money was one easy way to get over an attack of blues, and I was often homesick. Yet I must confess I liked that sort of life; I liked the freedom, the sense of adventure and the lack of responsibility. But there were drawbacks. It was cold lots of times, and I did not always have enough food, although no one had to go empty in the West.

If you got to a water tank and were put off by the train crew, you would walk to town, a mile or so away, and if you had no money, you would go to a back door and say that you were hungry. In her life my mother must have fed thousands out our way. Any time you knocked at a back door out West and explained that you were on the move, looking for work, you got something to eat; maybe just bread and butter, maybe a few slices of cold meat. No one ever felt a need to blush in those days for eating such a meal. When you had eaten and rolled a cigarette, you could feel a happy glow inside at the thought of the swell job you might get in the next town. Ah, but what a tough life that is in cold weather!

By identifying myself sometimes, I was allowed to ride in a caboose. On top of a freight train on a down grade, I've turned a brake wheel many a time. A few times I was allowed to climb up in the engine cab, sit on the fireman's side, ring the bell and look ahead for him. However, a lot of train crews were strict; on certain divisions they had to be or lose their jobs. When the engine was stopped, with brake sticks in their hands, they'd hunt the train from end to end for all manner of unofficial riders. Then they would try to pull out and leave us. If they succeeded, all of us castaways would congregate at the water tank; it was surprising sometimes to see what a variety of men had been hidden aboard.

Sometimes I was alone, again I'd be in the company of another machinist or a boiler maker. Frequently there would be other roving workmen, but also there would be men more difficult to classify; fellows with bloodshot, reckless eyes, sinister scars and tattoo marks. Invariably, however, there would be a few whiskered men in broken shoes

69

and ragged coats held together by safety pins or bits of string. Nevertheless, until another train came along, we would be thrown together in the free-masonry that embraces any group of wayfarers. We'd all rustle wood, and soon there would be a bonfire. If you had a nickel bag of tobacco and some papers, you did not dare to violate convention by smoking alone; any who lacked tobacco smoked with you. That was a swell arrangement; I didn't always have tobacco. We'd talk a while, but if, as sometimes happened, the conversation was dull, why, that was when it would seem worth while to take your knife out and carve your initials on a water-tank post.

I finally lost my tuba. There was not a lot of music in that instrument, but somehow I always enjoyed the big noise that I valved out of it; it seemed especially grand when any band I was a part of played the overture from William Tell. I'll have to retrace my route by ear to remember where I parted with my horn forever. Let me see: Cheyenne—big shops there—Rawlins, Rock Springs, Laramie and Ogden, Utah. That brings it back! I beat it into Ogden with another fellow. I saw the Union Pacific foreman there and he put me to work. I stayed six weeks that time, but roving had almost become a habit; box-car travel offered an easy escape from boredom. So, when this other fellow and I heard a lot of talk about the shops at Pocatello, Idaho, we started. I put my tuba in the custody of a conductor, gave him a cigar and asked him to see that it was delivered to the Oregon Short Line roundhouse in Pocatello. Well, the two of us arrived at last in Pocatello. Every minute of the time that I was awake I wished I had not come. The wind was blowing all the time. It seemed to me that there could be no other wind quite its equal in ferocity. I swear, it would blow gravel right in your face. In less than two weeks

I knew I had enough. I left Pocatello in a box car of a train of empties headed south.

I was brushing off the travel dust in Salt Lake City before I remembered that I had neglected to arrange for anybody to bring my tuba south. I hope whoever became its master learned to play it sweetly.

In Salt Lake City I got a job in the shops of the Denver & Rio Grande Western Railroad. That was in 1900. There was a friend from Ellis, a man named Sam Smith, who was the roundhouse foreman. He fixed it so I got thirty cents an hour. He liked the way I worked, and I liked him and I liked the shop. Moreover, I liked Salt Lake City. I began to go around a lot, to Saltair Pavilion on the shore of the lake to swim and dance. I had made up my mind I was through with roving. I guess when I left my tuba I likewise left behind a certain frame of mind.

I worked a year and saved my money to the best of my ability. I was often dreadfully lonesome. Every time I saw a railroad train moving eastward I wished myself aboard it. Every time I heard a locomotive mournfully whistling "who, who-oo-oo, who-oo-oo who" I knew the answer to my lonesomeness: Della Forker. We exchanged letters faithfully. She never wavered during that time when I was a wandering mechanic; she knew why I was roving, knew that she was completely interwoven with my ambitions.

I cherished all her letters and when I was blue I cured myself by reading them and inhaling their faint perfume. I was twenty-six. A prospective bridegroom could not return for his wedding in a box car or caboose; I had bought a derby hat and other appropriate clothes, but I still had to go on saving. Then, at last, I was able to write her that I was coming home and asked her to fix a day for the ceremony, reporting that I had enough money for expenses and to tide us over to the next payday. I got passes East, over the D. & R. G. W., to Denver; for the return trip it was good for "W. P. Chrysler & wife." But there was no chance of getting a pass for the journey between Denver and my home town over the Union Pacific, regardless of the years I had worked for that line. So it happened that when I reached Denver I stood before a railroad station window and for the first time in my life bought a railroad ticket. On its face, however, that ticket bore a word that in several homesick years had become entirely glamorous: Ellis.

We were married in the Methodist Church. My wife's mother had died and so it was a quiet wedding, just our two families. We caught the midnight train for Denver. Believe me, I had settled down.

We began our married life in Salt Lake City with sixty dollars; that was every cent I had. As a roundhouse mechanic, I was getting thirty cents an hour, three dollars for a ten-hour day. Whenever I could pile up some overtime, I figured I was lucky. Through the summer we lived in a little house that we had rented furnished and watched the completion of a row of terraced flats. Before the builders had finished them, we had rented one of these. When it was ready, we moved in with $170 worth of furniture that I had signed up to buy on time.

I had more ambition then than ever. I had been studying, carrying on a course in electrical engineering by mail through The International Correspondence Schools. I had heard about that from Bill Kilpatrick, an Ellis boy who had moved to Salt Lake City and served his apprenticeship out there. When he had told me what he was doing to get a technical education, I had said, "I'm going to do that too."

I had what might be called a lucky break in Utah. Out there the Mormons pay their tithes twice in every year, and tithing time is a festival period; during the autumn tithing week thousands of Mormons would be on the move, bringing one tenth of all they had produced in cash, calves, lambs, eggs, hams, vegetables, fruits, or other things to officials of their church. All this made a traffic problem for the railroads in the state; the D. & R. G. W. was busy hauling Mormon passengers and hauling a freight of tithes. It happened that they had to send a special train up what was called the Tintic Branch to bring in passengers from the mountains who wished to pay their tithes in Salt Lake City.

The road was short of motive power in those days, and to haul the special on its round trip in the morning, it was decided to use an engine that would be needed in the afternoon to take out the train to Denver. This through train was scheduled to leave Salt Lake City at three P. M.

I was standing at the register book in the roundhouse, taking off some work, when I saw the master mechanic, John Hickey, come tearing into the roundhouse waving a telegram at Sam Smith, the roundhouse foreman. Mr. Hickey was a dapper man who always came to work dressed as if to attend a wedding; his coat was a cutaway, his pants were striped and his hat an unblemished gray fedora. He was gray-haired, and to my mind, then, the perfect model of a gentleman. But this time he was in a lather.

"Smith, Engine 46 has blown out a back cylinder head on that special run. What in the name of——"

"That's the only engine you got," said Smith, "that can take that Denver train out of here."

"I know that," said Hickey. "The question is: Can we get her repaired in time?"

"Well, I got a young fellow here I think can do the job."

They came over to me then. Hickey knew me. He always called me "Crissler." He was puffing from his hurry. "Criss-

73

ler, can you put a back cylinder head on No. 46 and have her ready for the through trip?"

"If anybody can," I said, "I can."

"That's the spirit, Crissler."

"You'll have to give me two helpers."

"Fine, fine! . . . Smith, give him all the help he wants." Then Hickey dashed away and Smith asked: "What do you think? Can you do it?"

"Well, I didn't say I could; I said, 'If anybody can, I can'."

I picked my helpers then, got my wrenches and other tools and laid them beside the roundhouse pit where I would have to do this job. Then I went to the machine shop and loaded into a hand truck a new back cylinder head, wrist pins, bolts, studs and other things I thought I might need. I trucked this over to the roundhouse pit and checked it over to make sure I had everything I possibly could need. Then I took my two helpers down to the coal chute where the crippled locomotive would pause first when she arrived.

Naturally, she was operating only on one side when she rolled in; the broken side that needed my attention was idle, and so, even before she stopped, I was working on her, stripping off nuts and crossheads as I walked beside her. As the cripple puff, puff, puffed unevenly toward the ashpit, I kept busy with my wrench.

When the fire was dropped out of her, it all but scorched my shins. I never stopped and I kept my helpers going fast. When I first touched her at the coal chute, it was just past noon—ten past to be exact, but the whistle meant nothing to me that day. Smith, the roundhouse foreman, went to my home, explained the situation to my worried wife and waited while she packed a dinner pail for me.

Two hours and forty minutes after I began the job, I yelled to Smith, "You can take her away; she's ready." It was

74

ten minutes to three and the Denver train pulled out on time.

Old Man Hickey watched her go, his watch in his hand. I think he had been praying to that watch all the time I worked. But when she passed from sight, he came to where I stood wiping my face with a piece of waste.

"Crissler, I thought the Denver train was doomed to be at least an hour and a half late. I had no idea you'd get that engine out of here in time. I wouldn't have believed anybody who told me a mechanic could do a job like that in so short a time."

Of course, I glowed; that kind of praise is better than meat and drink for any man. But old man Hickey was not finished:

"You know the wages you fellows get are fixed. If I could boost your pay, I would." He thought a moment; then he beamed, "I'll tell you, Crissler, there is something I can do for you. You can have the rest of the afternoon off." It was three o'clock.

I did not go home. I sat on the side of the pit, ate to the bottom of my dinner pail, smoked my cigarette, walked around for fifteen minutes and then went back to work. I felt grand; I wasn't going to sacrifice a minute of my feeling of triumph.

It must have been about five months later that word was sent for me to come to the master mechanic's office. I wasn't "Crissler" any longer. As I walked in, John Hickey said, "Walter, do you think you can hold down the job of foreman over in the roundhouse?"

"Sure I can. But what's going to become of Mr. Smith?"

"We've got another better job for Smith. So I'd like to give you this job as roundhouse foreman."

Thereafter I had an office; just a little hole in the wall compared with some I've seen, but it contained a dinky roll-

75

top desk with a telephone. I was foreman over about ninety men.

The union had a rule about such matters. In those days, when a man accepted a foremanship, he was held to be on "the company's side." Therefore, he could not continue his membership in the union. Instead he was given a "withdrawal card." If I lost my job, of course, I could get back in the union. But I did not mean to lose it; at home we needed all the extra money I could make. Just about that time, our first child was born, Thelma; she who was to become Mrs. Byron Foy.

Even so, before I had been foreman at the roundhouse very long, I made John Hickey mad.

·IV·

A CHANCE MEETING IN CHICAGO

1908

"I Spent Four Days Hanging Around The Show"

· IV ·

A CHANCE MEETING IN
CHICAGO

I KNEW what was coming, the instant I discovered it was not the dispatcher on the wire; with a cold feeling in my stomach, I recognized the voice that rasped through the intercommunicating telephone receiver as that of Mr. Hickey's clerk. For several days I had been fearful of a summons from the general master mechanic.

You do not need to drown to have much of your past life reel through your mind in just a single second. Jobs were scarce; and the sudden fear that you are about to lose your job may do that to you if you are young—I was twenty-seven—and constant in your solicitude for a wife and baby. I had a wife, so pretty that I was swollen with pride any time we appeared together; a loyal and devoted wife who cooked, cleaned, washed and nursed through longer hours than I worked. She was the one who managed so the pay check stretched through the month. We both felt that we were lucky to have ninety dollars a month. The thought of losing what we had made me feel that I was encountering calamity when the clerk spoke: "Mr. Hickey wants to see you in his office."

My own little office meant much to me. I had authority. I was the boss of scores of men—fellows like myself who understood metal and machines. In it, beside my small desk, was a pot-bellied stove, a relic of a time when every railroad coach was heated with one of its cast-iron species. Except on rare days, this was just a target for the tobacco juice of my visitors. There were several extra chairs of wood, their sheen darkened because of the greasy overalls of those who sat in them. Anyone who stepped in to see the roundhouse foreman stood, not on bare boards or cinders but on an oilcloth mat. However, Mr. Hickey's office was much finer. He was the boss of thousands, and his authority extended all over the railroad, over division master mechanics, over scores of foremen, over swarms of machinists, over engineers and firemen. There was a carpet on the floor of Mr. Hickey's office.

That was the carpet I was heading for as I started out of the roundhouse to obey the summons. From behind the row of levers in the switchman's tower, an arm was raised to wave to me. I had many friends around the yards, I waved back, not too gaily. I was a forceful, snappy young fellow, quick-tempered. That was the trouble. A few days before, I had opened and read a letter from the general master mechanic. I have forgotten now what act or oversight of mine had caused him to write this rebuke, but I remember well how quickly I got mad. A sassy letter from the boss, eh? Well, I could write a sassy letter too. Because I was young, he need not think he could take my hide off. My trouble was youthful sensitiveness. What I could not understand as I crunched along the path of cinders towards the offices was what had impelled him to wait three or four days. I know that in that time I had come to realize two things: that Mr. Hickey had both cause to rebuke me and cause to feel outraged for my lack of respect, as shown in my reply. Well, if I was going to get it in the neck, I

A CHANCE MEETING IN CHICAGO

was not going to whimper. I clamped my teeth, squared my shoulders and opened the boss's door.

"Hello Walt. Sit down. I have been looking at some drawings of a new locomotive. A monster, isn't it?" Mr. Hickey had me off guard then. He chatted on and on until, I suppose, he saw that I was relaxed.

"Walt, you're a good boy. You're a hard worker. I don't know a better mechanic. You've got courage too. But there are some other things I feel I have to say to you. Four or five months ago I made you foreman at the roundhouse, made you responsible for the motive power, and for something else: For the men, for the work they do."

I knew it was coming then, but I was making up my mind to take whatever Mr. Hickey cared to say; had he roared, I would have roared louder; instead he wore me down with kind and gentle words.

"Walt, I know you pretty well. Right after you went to work, I fixed my eye on you. Remember when we bought those four new cross-compound engines? I was worried about their valves. Where would we get a man to set them? The Baldwin man assured me it would be no problem. He said we had a kid in the roundhouse who knew as much about the engines as he did. He told me how you learned about those cross-compounds and their complicated valves."

That floored me. When this Baldwin man had come to Salt Lake City to set up these engines, I had just about lived with him. I had worked with him by day, and after supper had gone to his hotel to sit with him until ten or eleven at night, asking questions until I nearly tired him out. When he had gone East, I had been the only mechanic who could set those engines' valves. Most of the parts were similar to other locomotives, but the valve motion was complicated. Sometimes a rock thrown up from the road bed would strike and bend a little eccentric rod, and the engine would go lame, a mysterious thing to everybody else. Many times a call boy came for me at night to fix one of those cross-compounds in a hurry. I'd get up, go down to the roundhouse, take off the bent rod, straighten it up and have the engine right all within an hour. Then the night man would say, "Kid, that's quick work—too quick, in fact. Put in for ten hours' overtime, but go on home to bed. Then you can get a full day's work tomorrow."

Maybe Mr. Hickey even knew about that extra overtime; I don't know. Certainly, he knew plenty about human beings. There isn't one of us who won't listen carefully to a sermon that begins with praise of our work or something else that we take pride in. You can bet, I listened that day.

"You know, Walt, you've got a future. I don't want to see you throw it away just because your feelings get hurt now and then. Let me tell you this: now and then, I get a letter that makes me boil with rage. You know what I do?"

Mr. Hickey reached deep into his roll-top desk, so that his glossy cuff protruded for almost its length; from a small drawer beneath the pigeonholes he pulled out a sheet of fingermarked paper. I saw that it was the letter I had written. I was red to the roots of my hair. "Walt, there is where I put letters that make me mad. I leave them there three or four days until I have calmed down. When I am sure"—Mr. Hickey smiled on me then—"I take them out and read them over."

I don't believe I could have stood it if he had read my letter aloud just then; happily, he simply laid it down between us and kept on talking, gently:

"If you had put my letter in a drawer until you cooled off, Walt, you'd have dealt with it much more soundly; you would have been fair to me and fair to yourself. Don't you see? Now, boy, you remember what I've told you."

I apologized right then; words of contrition poured out of me the way potatoes do when you spill the barrel.

Since that day I've never answered any letter while in a passion. Oh, I've gotten mad and pounded my fist on a table when talking face to face, but I never have lost my temper on paper. God knows, I have received letters that seemed to tear my heart out, but those letters I have always filed in the bottom drawer. Just the act of pulling it open brings a thought of old man Hickey and cools me down.

When I refer to Mr. Hickey as "old," it is with affection; he was the "old man" simply because he was the boss, the one whose words of praise, of sympathetic understanding, gave more lasting satisfaction than my pay checks. Now, looking backward over the course I have traveled, I recall him as one of my best teachers, a trainer who showed me how to curb some traits of temper that well might have sidetracked me, or even caused derailment.

I had been roundhouse foreman just about a year when, one day, there came a telegram from Trinidad, Colorado, that got me all excited. It was signed by H. C. Van Buskirk, superintendent of motive power of the Colorado & Southern, a road that ran from Denver down to Texline, Texas, where it was linked with the Fort Worth & Denver City Railroad. In the telegram, Van Buskirk offered me a job as general foreman of the Colorado & Southern's shops at Trinidad. Fifteen dollars more a month! But I did not know Van Buskirk, never had heard of him. I tore around for several hours, hardly knowing where I stood at any time. Maybe Mr. Hickey could set me straight.

"What can I do for you, Walt? Sit down."

I pulled out the telegram. "I've got something here that's bothering me an awful lot."

Mr. Hickey read the telegram, peered at me, read the telegram again, then peered back. "Well, Walt, this is a fine opportunity, getting a general foremanship when you are only—let me see—is it thirty?" He grinned. I think he suspected the truth—that I was just past twenty-eight.

"But I don't know Mr. Van Buskirk, and yet he wires for me."

"I happen to know him. Probably he heard from somebody that you were a hustler and a good mechanic. I suppose he has a tough job of some kind that he wants cleaned up."

We talked for half an hour and the old man expanded. He had begun by serving an apprenticeship with the Cuyahoga Machine Works at Cleveland, Ohio. He had a short term as machinist, became a locomotive engineer, then became a foreman of engine repairs with the Burlington. In '73 he had become master mechanic of the Sheboygan & Fond du Lac Railroad.

"So you see, Walt, after a general foremanship, the next step is master mechanic somewhere."

"Gee, Mr. Hickey! But you went to college."

"Surely; in Toronto, Upper Canada College, before I became an apprentice. But you don't have to go to college to get an education. Keep on with your correspondence courses. You'll learn faster and better than most fellows, because you are getting it through your fingers and your eyes, instead of through your ears. What is this course you're taking? An electrical-mechanical engineering course?"

"Yes, sir. I'm studying drafting now. But, listen, I'd like to stay here. I've been happy. I ——"

"You are a hustler, and I'd hate like the devil to lose you. But, you know, our general foreman here is an excellent man. I expect he'll hold his job until I die or get fired. Do you want to wait ten or fifteen years? I never hope to have a better roundhouse foreman. That job is yours as long as you want it."

"But, Mr. Hickey, I want advice."

"Take the job, Walt! It's a great opportunity for you. You're learning how to swing authority while you're young. Don't stop!" Then he dampered down his enthusiasm a trifle: "I am telling you that if I were in your shoes I'd take the job. I should regret to see you let a fine opportunity slide by just because you are comfortable in a job that you have mastered. Don't be afraid of your future."

"I ain't afraid, but I got a wife and baby."

"You got a splendid wife. Talk to her. Then let me know. And good luck!" He waved his arm widely, as conductors do when they hold a lantern in their hand and signal to the engineer to go ahead.

When I got to the flat, my wife put the dinner on the table and we talked as we ate, while Thelma in her high chair clattered a spoon against its wooden tray.

"What do you say, Della? Fifteen dollars means fifty cents every day in the month. It won't cost much to move. The furniture will go half rate and we'll have passes, but Trinidad is hundreds of miles away."

"Dad, you are the one to say. I won't fret or worry, whatever comes. Certainly we could use that money." Saying this, she wrapped her arms around the child. I had her answer.

"Then we'll move."

Once it was the Santa Fe Trail, made glamorous by the feet, the hoofs and creaking wheels of all that had marched and rolled along it as part of the pageantry of American history. When I first walked on the trail, what my feet

85

touched had become fixed by stones, boards and bricks into the main street of Trinidad, zigzagging down the hillside.

I was out of overalls in Trinidad and I meant to stay out. What I would wear to work was the oldest suit I had; it was worn and spotted, but it was good enough to distinguish me as one who worked entirely with his head. My superior, the master mechanic of the division, was a man of sixty-five or so, named H. Geigoldt. I grew fond of him, but the old man had slight strength to do his work. I had to work just that much harder in my role of general foreman of the shops.

I had complete charge of repairing locomotives, not only the roundhouse jobs of temporary repairs between scheduled runs but also the overhauling.

When we overhauled an engine, we took it all apart and rebuilt it. Besides, I had charge of keeping all our freight cars in repair, and I built some new cars too. The shops had been in a run-down condition when I came, and this, of course, was reflected in the state of the railroad's motive power.

I worked like a dog for more than a year. I rarely got enough hours in bed, and at the table I bolted my meals, thinking constantly of all the problems of my job. I was far below my normal physical state, but the shops and the roundhouse were a whole lot better than when I came; so was nearly all the motive power. One day Mr. Van Buskirk, the superintendent of motive power, walked with me through the shops. I had been there as general foreman, then, about one year and nine months, and I could take pride in what we saw. In the roundhouse I had put a foreman I had picked for loyalty, character and ability. He was a big, tall, fine-looking fellow with a great shock of hair, and after he had taken charge I no longer had any roundhouse worries. I mention this because, as I look back, it seems to me that one of my best skills has been a faculty of selecting men wisely.

"Let's go to your office. I want to talk with you." Van Buskirk spoke solemnly, and for just a second I asked myself, "What could be wrong?"

"Walter, this is what I want to ask: Can you run the job of master mechanic?"

"Of course I can run it. But say, what's going to happen to Mr. Geigoldt? If you are going to fire that old man to give me his job, I won't take it."

"Now don't get excited, Walt. You know Mr. Geigoldt is getting pretty old. Out of Denver we got a little short division and we are going to move him up there, so he can take it easy. This job takes too much out of him, and we want to make you master mechanic."

In a little while, Mr. Geigoldt came to me with his hand outstretched, smiling. "I knew it first," he said. "Congratulations." A couple of weeks later he moved away and I was master mechanic of the two divisions extending out of Trinidad.

Van Buskirk had made it clear just what we had to do: The Colorado & Southern was to be built up until it was a first-class railroad. You do not tolerate late trains on a first-class road, and I had a problem that ran through twenty-four hours of every day, keeping our trains on time. Responsibility, I was learning, is something that weighs more heavily than iron. Probably there were a thousand men—all the engine crews, the shopmen, the carmen and the roundhouse fellows over several hundred miles of track —who were referring to me then as "the old man," though I was just under thirty. Being young, of course, was what made it all such great fun. But there was another reward. For what I was doing I was paid $140 a month.

I had a friend out there named Cotter—George Cotter—who was one of a family of railroad men. George was made superintendent at Trinidad just about the time I came there as general foreman. I used to look at him and wish deep inside of me that I had gone to college. As a railroad mechanical man I took it for granted that a man as young as he was with so much authority on the administrative side of the railroad had a college background. His cultured speech, his ease of manner anywhere caused me to assume this, I suppose. Well, I plugged all the harder at my correspondence courses, so as to overcome my handicap. It was not for years that I discovered George Cotter left school when he was fourteen, became a railroad telegraph messenger, then an operator; from that point on, his rise was like that of his brother—train dispatcher, chief dispatcher, train-master and then division superintendent. As I look back, it becomes quite plain that railroads, railroad work, had been George Cotter's college; and the work had given him a polish too.

One time he came to my office over the shops and cussed a time or two.

"What's the matter?"

"Alkali! I've got to do something about the well out there beyond the watershed. I've had my roadmaster there most of the time to keep that shallow well working at all, and the water from it has so much alkali in solution—well, nobody knows better than you what it is doing to the locomotives."

Alkali was a problem at some points on most Western railroads. My very first work in the Ellis shops, when I was a sweeper, was lugging boiler tubes from the shops out to a shed where we rattled them around until that hard deposit

88

was flaked off. We thought it was a problem in Western Kansas, but in the shops at Trinidad it was a nightmare.

"Walt, there's sweet water down there below the watershed, but it is deeper in the earth than we can reach with any ordinary pump. Maybe you've got some idea how we can get water out of a real deep well. If you can tell me how, you'll have solved my biggest problem, and yours as well."

"George, have you ever heard of a submerged well?"

"A what kind of a well?"

"Submerged." I repeated the word with just that trace of emphasis that would suggest that I supposed everybody had heard about submerged wells. As it happened, the only time I ever had heard of one was in an article which I had read several years before. Fortunately, though, whenever I did read about a mechanical device, I read it with pains, to understand what I was reading.

"Walt, if you could make me a well like that, and if it worked—— Go on, tell me more."

I never did tell him where I got my information, but I explained the principle while we went to my house to eat.

"You don't need an ordinary pump at all; you do need an air compressor and a steam boiler to run it. You put a pipe down into your casing just the way a kid sticks a straw in a sodawater glass, only you do not suck; you blow. You force air down that submerged pipe, and the air pushes the water up in the casing. Of course, it all has to be figured out carefully, but that won't be hard, once we know the depth of the well."

Cotter was pounding on the table in his delight. "My gosh, if we could make it work —— Say, where did you ever hear of a thing like that?"

"Oh, I hear about lots of things."

89

"Well, will you do it for me?"

"Sure." I had never even seen one of the things.

First I got estimates on the cost of a compressor, then some bids on the pipe. We knew from the start that the water we were after was about 600 feet down. When I made up an estimate, the total was $9500, and that was a lot of money. However, George got approval for the expenditure, and I was told to go and supervise the job.

We drilled the well 600 feet and cased it to a depth of 480 feet; we had a bottom of water then that seemed to have a constant level. We had a seventy-five-foot length of pipe in which a lot of three-quarter-inch holes had been cut, and this was to be at the bottom of the submerged pipe through which we would blow our air against the water. That was all there was to it, except to build a concrete foundation and install the steam boiler and the compressor.

Finally, when the submerged well was within a week of being completed, I got a telegram from Cotter that he was arriving, to remain with me until the job was finished. I looked forward to his coming, because any time spent with George was fun. However, when he came, I felt less at ease than I had ever felt before; he was in a private car, attended by a staff of roadmasters, bridge-construction superintendents and some others, including all the officers of the division. I was still a green Kansan, a small-town fellow. Through all my years I had given myself so completely to my work that there were a lot of things I did not know.

"We're having luncheon in the car, Walt."

"Thanks, George, but I can't leave this job right now. I'll watch these fellows ——"

"Oh, come on! You got to eat somewhere."

"I got my lunch basket. See you after a bit."

Cotter asked me to that private car of his three times

the day he came. Always I had some reason for not going: I was dirty and greasy from monkeying with the drilling machine, or I did not want to stop to change my clothes, or I had to get some sleep. I was using all my imagination to keep myself supplied with reasons for not going into the private car. The truth was that I was scared—scared to enter, because I thought I did not know how to act. I had never been in a private car.

On the second day of this, George came to me at noon and took me by the arm. Then somebody, an enormous Irish roadmaster, took me by the other.

"Come on to lunch." They had moved me four steps before I got my mouth open to say I had my lunch right there in my basket.

"Come on." There was something in Cotter's blue eyes that seemed to mean "no fooling." So I went along, as nervous and excited as if they were trying to shove me down my well.

"Let me go and change my clothes."

"Ah, the hell with your clothes! Get in the car." They boosted me aboard.

In a little while I was sitting before a tablecloth so white and spotless it was a challenge to every slightest move I made in my greasy well-drilling clothes. It seemed to me that the rolling of the eyeballs of the colored waiters— these were the first I had encountered—was a restless activity designed by them the more quickly to catch me in some dreadful error of deportment. Then the worst happened!

The waiter placed in front of me a plate that bore a pair of steaming objects about the size of my finger. Incredibly they appeared to be wrapped in corn husks, tied at the ends with string. I was as alert as a prairie chicken trying to select the moment to abandon cover and fly up in a hunter's face. I stole looks at the others in vain; George, always carefully groomed, was using his hands to gesture while he talked about Fort Worth, and the Irish roadmaster, after sipping water, took forever to preen his mustache. All the gentlemen were slow to start. I could not cope with such leisure. I had to get back to work. So I took my knife and fork, slashed off an end and tried to eat it.

The lot of them were Irish, and they could not stand it any longer. They roared with laughter. In his merriment, tears ran down George's rosy cheeks. He had planned to stump me with those hot tamales. Red-faced, I cleaned my plate somehow without eating any more corn husks. All I could think of was to get out of that place; but they did not let me go until George, swell fellow that he was, who knew my quick temper was a reflex of my sensitiveness, was sure that I had not been wounded by the laughter.

At the well rig that afternoon, I kept living through the hell of seeing those unknown objects on my plate, of feeling hideously out of place and being ignorant about so many things that women rate as important. I began to get my wife's slant on certain aspects of living. She had never nagged me once, but I knew that back in Ellis, where all the girls went in heavily for refinement, she had eaten at a table somewhat differently served than when she had just me to feed. Table manners? The appetite a machinist brings home when the noon whistle blows was never meant to suffer any kind of waiting. Put the food on the table and let a man eat is manners when he is ravenous from working hard and has to get back to a job before another whistle blows.

Yet I realized, after that first experience in a private car, that there were a lot of things in the world besides machinery and men. I went back to eat with George that night, and for the balance of the week I ate all my meals there, including the one which was in celebration of the completion of the submerged well. It worked right from the start, because the hydraulic calculations had been sound. To get good sweet water out of it, all that was required was to turn a valve. When this was done the first time, while George and his crowd looked on, a bubbling geyser shot up in the air, forty feet or more.

No alkali in that water!

Then George got a job with greater scope, one where he had a lot more authority and more money; he was appointed general superintendent of the Fort Worth & Denver City. This road coupled on to ours at Texline, Texas, and extended on to Fort Worth and Dallas. Before he left, he came to see me.

"Walt, why don't you come down there with me? You are just the kind of fellow I can work with, and down in Texas I've got a shop problem I'd like to have you tackle."

"You see how you like it first, George."

Three months after Cotter left, he wired me from Fort Worth, asking me to meet him in Childress, Texas, a little village about 300 miles or so from Trinidad. It is south of the Red River, close to the southwest corner of Oklahoma. George met me there.

"Last week our shop burned down at Clarendon," he began. "It was put there when the road was built, but the site was badly chosen. This is a much more strategic spot, here at Childress. We can have a longer division and save a lot in operations. Now, Walt, I want you to come down here and build this shop the way you think a shop ought to be. And then you run it. You'll be the master mechanic of the division."

"Gee, I'd like better than anything to build a shop. I

got some ideas, just from seeing poor ones, but ——"

"Come on, what do you say?"

"I'll have to put this up to Della."

"All right. Tell her you get twenty dollars more a month."

"George, I want to come. But you got to admit that in its present state this is a —— Say, look at all this red clay dust on my pants and shoes, and wait'll you see your face!"

We walked around the small town, just a village then, and I could find only one house for rent. It was a four-room farmhouse, an unpainted box out in the middle of an eight-acre cornfield. This was in the fall of the year, and to reach that house George and I walked through a field of corn-stalks to have a talk with the farmer. There was literally nothing in that house to make life easier for a woman. If I would pay ten dollars a month, the farmer was willing to move his family into another little house elsewhere on the farm. The only water supply near the house was a well, and the water from that had a sulphurous taste; it was a spa in embryo. If we stayed there we would have to haul our drinking water from somewhere.

I went back to Trinidad, itching in my soul for the chance to build the new shops at Childress, but I did not see how I could ask my wife to take her baby into such a shelter.

"A terrible little house, Della. Right out in a cornfield. You've got friends here now and we're pretty comfortable. Of course we can live cheaper than we can live in Trinidad, and I'll get twenty dollars more a month. Best of all, it is an opportunity; later on, it will be worth something for me to be able to say I built the shops at Childress. Did I tell you about that gyp water? You wouldn't dare let the baby drink a drop of it. That house out in a cornfield ——"

94

"Dad, if you think that is the place for us to go, don't worry about me. I'll be happy anywhere you think you ought to be to get ahead. " There was never a time when my wife batted an eye to keep me staying on in any place on her account. I've had friends whose wives literally spoiled their careers just by their whines and chronic kicking. Suppose sometime my wife had said, "No, I won't expose my child to the danger of living in such a place. I think you are foolish and selfish to try to drag me down to such a hole." Well, then, I would have stayed in Trinidad, or Salt Lake City, or Ellis. Probably I'd be there yet, but I'd be pretty wistful. Nothing in my life has given me more cause for pride and satisfaction than the way my wife had faith in me from the very first, through all those years when I was a grease-stained roundhouse mechanic. So we went to Childress, down in Texas.

The time-payment furniture was getting shabbier with each move we made. In the house at Childress we had the rug turned, so that the place most badly worn was underneath the bed. It had not been good furniture when we bought it in Salt Lake City for $170, but after long journeys in freight cars, in addition to the normal wear and tear, it was getting pretty awful. Yet I never heard my wife say, "This is not the sort of furniture I used to have in Ellis."

Well, I worked like a dog through the remainder of the fall and half the winter, getting the new shops erected and equipped. Then one day soon after they were completed, out of a clear sky I got a telegram from John E. Chisholm, at Oelwein, Iowa. He offered me his job as master mechanic on the Chicago Great Western Railroad. He was getting a promotion to the job of general master mechanic of the road. The job paid $200 a month, forty dollars more than I was getting, but there were other important angles. Chis-

holm and I had become friends in the West. At that time
he had bragged to me about the amazing equipment in those
Oelwein shops—transfer tables on which an engine could
be treated as a toy, and—something quite wonderful then
—decent washrooms and toilets for the men. We were still
drinking out of a common bucket at Childress, and the only
washing facilities the railroad had allowed was just the sort
of trough that I had used back in the Ellis days.

I sent off a wire to George Cotter at Fort Worth, telling
him that an exceptionally fine job had been offered to me,
that I had to accept at once or turn it down. I could not
get away myself to talk with George. He was the general
superintendent, but he was also my friend; so I said in my
wire that I would appreciate it if he would come up from
Fort Worth on the night train and talk it over. And George
came. He was grand.

"How can I turn this thing down, George? I hate to
leave you, but ——"

"Walt, I have to agree. It is a real opportunity. I could
pay you $200 a month, but not any more, and up there in
Oelwein you will be starting at $200. Those shops must be
fine, and of course it will be a whole lot better in a nice,
bustling town for Della. But who can I put in your place?"

"I got your man, George. The general foreman of the
shops. You don't know George Little as well as you know
me, but you can bet I know him. I made him a roundhouse
foreman at Trinidad, and he has been coming right along
behind me, job after job."

After that, I hustled over to the dispatcher's office and
sent a telegram to Chisholm, accepting the job and telling
him to expect me in about a week.

The chief dispatcher read my message, not with his eyes
but with his ears, as the words were being sent by a tele-

graph operator.

"Say, Walter! You are really leaving? Hey, can I rent that house you're living in? You know, I've had my wife here three months and we are boarding in a terrible place. How about it?"

"You can get the house if you will buy my furniture."

"Let's go over and look at it."

We got in a buggy and drove across the railroad tracks, through the thick red dust, across the cornfield to that forlorn and bleak-looking house. The baby was asleep when we tiptoed into the bedroom to appraise the stuff in there. We made a deal. For $100 I sold him everything except the silverware, table linens, bed sheets and some other personal things. But he got all the furniture and kitchenware. Five days later he was in the house and Della, Thelma and I were traveling northward; except for the baby carriage and a small suitcase, all we had was packed in one big box. All, that is, except $500 we had saved while living there in Childress.

"It'll be a much better place for you," I was telling my wife when we rolled out of Texas on a balmy day in February. "Oelwein is a town of almost 6000 people. It's a good railroad town. Everything considered, it's time we got you to a place where there will be some doctors handy."

We arrived there in the morning, stepping off the train into an Arctic region incased in snow and ice to a depth of eighteen inches. In the clothes we had been wearing down in Texas we began to shiver. I got the baby carriage from the baggageman, and when the baby was tucked in and wrapped with blankets, we set out for the hotel. I pushed the baby carriage, and once I slipped and fell.

After we had eaten breakfast and were established in a hotel room, I started for the job; on the way I saw what

97

would be a new responsibility of mine—great snowplows bucking and churning their way through the white mounds that were making all trains late; but, nevertheless, the trains were running.

Chisholm took me right to the shops, and I was thrilled to the marrow. I forgot all about the cold. They were the biggest shops I had ever seen. Sixteen or eighteen locomotives could be hauled inside of them. In the winter darkness they were brilliantly illuminated with the sputtering bluish arc lamps. There were great cranes aloft that could lift a locomotive in their chains. Everything was marvelous, and when I saw the transfer tables I felt like applauding. Best of all, everything in those shops was to be in my charge. I did not worry for a second. It was a bigger job; but thanks to an abundance of self-confidence, I knew I could run it.

I rented a story-and-a-half frame house in Oelwein; it had a nice porch that could be shaded in the summer with morning-glory vines. The house was on a big lot, just about half an acre. So we began at once to plan a garden, almost a little farm, in the rear. There was an empty barn. Of course, we had to have new furniture; we bought it on time. We wanted to keep that $500 in a savings bank. A short time after we arrived in Oelwein, our second child, Bernice, was born, displacing Thelma as "the baby" of the family. Bernice, when she grew up, married Edgar William Garbisch.

I knew how to get along with men; I was strong and I knew how to be fair, but I was a mechanic and nobody ever questioned that. I could put the center valves on the ranges so that they were right, and only a few mechanics failed to ask for help when they had a job like that to do. A. B. Stickney, both a lawyer and a construction engineer, was the president of the Chicago Great Western; he had built the road, and his son, Samuel Crosby Stickney, was vice-president and general manager. Sam Stickney was a splendid engineer, a graduate of Massachusetts Institute of Technology. All along the line of that road I had friends. In 1936, years after I left that job in Oelwein, a locomotive engineer I had known out there came to my office in the Chrysler Building. What he wanted me to do that day was to look down into the street, so I could see that he was riding in a Plymouth car.

Within a year and three months after I arrived in Iowa, John Chisholm left the railroad and I was promoted to his place as general master mechanic. Three months after that my title changed again: I was the superintendent of motive power. Over the whole railroad from Chicago to Oelwein, Oelwein to Minneapolis, I was in charge of engineers, firemen, carmen, shopmen, roundhouse men, and others. That took me up on the staff as high as a man could go mechanically in railroad service; of course, there were bigger railroads. I was learning plenty and still seething with ambition. My pay by that time was $350.

Frequently I had to travel over to Chicago on business, but in 1908 I went to Chicago to see the automobile show. That is where it happened. I saw this Locomobile touring car; it was painted ivory white and the cushions and trim were red. The top was khaki, supported on wood bows. Straps ran from that top to anchorages on either side of the hood. On the running board there was a handsome tool box that my fingers itched to open. Beside it was a tank of gas to feed the front head lamps; just behind the hood on either side of the cowling was an oil lamp, shaped quite like those on horse drawn carriages. I spent four days hanging around the show, held by that automobile as by a siren's song.

The price tag meant just what it said, as I found out by repeated inquiries: $5000 cash. I had $700. I must confess that I never stopped to ask myself if I should, if I could afford to go in hock to buy that car. All I asked myself was: Where could I raise the money?

· V ·

EXPERIMENTS WITH
HORSE-POWER

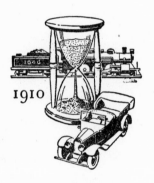

"What a Job I Could Do Here"

· V ·

EXPERIMENTS WITH
HORSE-POWER

ONE acquaintance of mine who had access to a lot of money was a gigantic fellow named Ralph Van Vechten, a brother of Carl Van Vechten, the writer; he was a banker, second vice-president of the Continental National Bank. Van was inches taller than six feet and weighed well over 200 pounds. He was a grand companion. Usually, our encounters were in a favored rendezvous of railroad officials, a loop cafe we entered by descending a flight of marble stairs from Madison Street into the basement of the Hotel Brevoort. Down there I lay in ambush for Van Vechten, and sure enough, he came.

"Van, this Locomobile model that has me hypnotized is the first touring car to have four doors. I'll bet you've seen it at the auto show—a creamy white, with red leather upholstery and a khaki top."

"You told me that this morning, Walt, and yesterday afternoon."

That was true; I had been worrying the life out of him for several days, trying to get him to lend me $4300 on my note. Every time I had tried to state an argument, he had blocked me by saying, "What about collateral?"

I did not have a thing that could be called collateral. The

$700 which was the total of my savings was to be used with the $4300 that Van steadily was refusing to lend me, to pay $5000 for that Lulu of an automobile. Hopelessly infatuated with the car I twisted logic and mustered feeble facts to buttress my case:

"Van, you know a lot about the transportation business; you do business with the railroads here in Chicago every day. Well, the automobile is the transportation business too. The railroads have made this a richer country, haven't they?"

"Surely."

"Well, then, just ask yourself what this country will be like when every individual has his private car and is able to travel anywhere. Some day ——"

"Go on, Walt, be sensible. You get $350 a month and you want to spend $5000 for an automobile." The impatient accent he put on the first syllable of that word was devastating to my cause.

"Listen, Van, I'll be making more money before long. I'll give you a mortgage on the car, if that's what you want."

"Walt, get somebody to sign the note with you and we might do business. That is, provided the co-signer has something besides pen and ink."

"You mean that, Van? If I get somebody else ——"

"Some substantial person, Walt. I like you, and if it was my money and you wanted it for anything less frivolous than an automobile, I'd feel like helping you out. But this is bank money you are trying to borrow. This is——"

"How about Bill Causey?" William Bowdoin Causey, a civil engineer and a Virginian, was then superintendent of the Chicago Great Western Railway's Oelwein-Chicago division. He lived in Chicago and was a close friend of Van Vechten; he was my friend too. He was to win distinction in the World War and afterward, when for four years he was the technical adviser of the Austrian Government. "Walt, if you can get Bill Causey to sign the note with you, maybe we can fix this thing up. Bill has a little money."

"All right, Van; I'll be at the bank in the morning and I'll have Bill with me. He's already told me he would go on my note."

That is how I raised the money to buy my first automobile. The only other times I had gone in debt had been in Salt Lake City and in Oelwein, to buy some furniture. Clearly, that car had a fascination for me that must have seemed to others the equivalent of madness. But I really meant it when I argued my case with Causey and with Van Vechten; I did not simply want a car to ride in; I wanted the machine so I could learn all about it. Why not? I was a machinist and these self-propelled vehicles were by all odds the most astonishing machines that had ever been offered to men.

Years later, when Van Vechten was one of a syndicate of bankers who felt that they were about to lose $50,000,000 in the Willys-Overland Company, he was glad he had made that loan to me; he told me so when the syndicate wanted to hire me to save their money. To induce me to go to work for them, they made a contract to pay me $1,000,000 a year for a term of two years. Van was a sport. In those later days he used to prod me in the ribs and tell, over and over, how I began to study automobiles by borrowing money from his bank on my note.

The barn in the back yard of our house in Oelwein was where we stored our garden tools, but more than half its space was cluttered with a lot of useless truck that had been left there by the former tenants of the premises. I began to clear this rubbish away, putting into a bonfire a dished buggy wheel, some dried-out, broken pieces of harness and bottles that had contained horse liniment. On that fire I dumped wheelbarrow loads of dust, straw and other litter, and did not stop until the barn was spick-and-span. By that time, my wife was excited by curiosity.

"I'm going to use it for a workshop."

"What are you going to make, dad?"

"Della, I've bought an automobile."

I told her all about it—that I had spent our cash reserve and gone in hock for more money than I would make in a year. She did not scold me, but it did seem to me that when she closed the kitchen door, it made a little more noise than usual; maybe she slammed it.

The automobile arrived in a freight car, anchored to the floor. I did not know how to run it, but I certainly was not going to allow another person to be the first behind its wheel. I arranged with a teamster to haul it to my house and put it in the barn. I cannot remember that I have ever been more jubilant than when Della, with Bernice in her arms and Thelma jumping up and down with excitement, saw me steer that horse-drawn car into the yard. If it had been a jewel of fantastic size, I could not have been more careful of it.

My wife was wild with enthusiasm then and wanted to take a ride immediately. But I put the car in the barn, and it stayed in there so long that she despaired of ever getting a ride. Sometimes she sat in it when I cranked up and let the engine run.

Night after night, I worked in the barn until it was time to go to bed, and some nights I did not leave the automobile until it was long past my bedtime. Saturday afternoons and all day on Sundays I worked on that car. I read automobile catalogues, I studied sketches and made still other sketches of my own. Most of the time, the innards were spread upon newspapers on the barn floor. There was no single function I did not study over and over. Finally, I proved to myself that I knew and understood it, because I had put it all together, had the engine tuned so that it was running like a watch.

"Dad, what is the use of having an automobile if we're never going to ride?"

"Now, don't be impatient, Della."

"Impatient! You've had the car three months and it's never been out of the barn."

It was a Saturday afternoon, and so hot that I had taken off my coat and had my sleeves rolled up. I finished eating. "In the barn three months, you say? Well, this afternoon she's coming out. Come look!"

By then the noise of the Chryslers' Locomobile engine was a commonplace in our neighborhood, but somehow the word was quickly spread that this was an exceptional occasion. I had a gallery of neighbors, as I cranked up, got behind the wheel, one hand devoted to steering and one to fiddling with that confounded sliding transmission lever. In those days, the steering mechanism was still being placed on the right side. She had a chain drive, of course, and that was what made her seem to growl and snarl every time I touched the transmission lever. I swear, you would have thought the car was ticklish, the way she winced, but the engine was purring, and when I looked behind, I could see that she was not smoking, much. Then I clamped my teeth on a fresh cigar and engaged the clutch.

The big touring car bucked like a mustang saddled for the first time. We shot forward; as some of the neighbors whooped and yelled, she bucked again and lurched into a ditch, rolled half a length farther and stalled, axle deep, in my neighbor's garden patch.

I had chewed up about one third of my cigar on that short run. I sent off for a man who had a team of horses. He came, the trace chains clinking against the stones in the road. The fetlocks of his horses were caked with mud.

"Careful where you hook those chains! Mind that paint! Be careful! Want to ruin that car?"

"Say, mister, I've hauled cars before and will again. Keep your shirt on. I'll hold these horses."

We pulled her out; I settled with the teamster and promised monetary satisfaction to my irate neighbor. I heard a few mocking laughs, and so I cranked her up, jumped in behind the throbbing wheel and started off. This time I got her into high and let her roll. All I was doing was to grip the wheel and steer. I had to turn at the corner, but rather than make those chains growl and clash, I let her go in high. I won't swear that only two wheels were touching the ground, but I want to testify that it felt that way. As we leveled off, we were at the edge of Oelwein, right in the country.

A few hundred yards ahead, I saw a cow emerging from behind an osage hedge that bordered a lane. She was headed for the road. I bulbed the horn until it had made its goose-like cry four or five times, but the cow, a poor rack of bones draped with yellow hide, kept right on her course and never changed her pace; nor did I change the pace of the automobile. I could not; all that I could do was to grip the wheel and steer, biting on my cigar until my teeth met inside of it.

Well, I missed the cow, though I was close enough to touch her. I missed few of the ruts and holes along that country road to the section line where there was an intersecting road, and there I turned again—a little slower on this turn—and rode another mile before turning onto the third side of a quadrangular course that I knew would bring me home. I fed more gas to the four-cylinder engine on the street that led toward home. On the basis of ratings today, that car would be said to have about eighty horse-power. As I came up the grade, the neighbors saw me riding fast, maybe twenty miles an hour. I stopped at the barn. My neighbors helped me push the car inside. I closed the doors and then discovered I was so tired I trembled. There was not a dry stitch of clothing on me; that perspiration came from nervousness and excitement. It was six o'clock in the evening then. I went into the house, stripped off my clothes, took a bath and got into bed. I was all in from that wild ride. Well, that's the way I learned to drive.

After that initiation, I made swift progress, until the Chrysler family was riding, not only on country roads but right through the bustling heart of Oelwein. My wife and I wore linen dusters on those rides. A great many times, though, I had that car apart, all its members spread upon the barn floor, and just as often had it assembled again, until I think I could have put it together, almost in the dark. However, I had other things to do.

The locomotive is the heart of a railroad; therefore, a sound performance by whoever held my job was vital to the Chicago Great Western Railway. Any time an engine broke down or a train was late, the fellow who had to bear the blame was the Superintendent of Motive Power, no matter who really was at fault. Consequently, I kept on the move; besides those splendid shops at Oelwein, there were others at Dubuque, Minneapolis, St. Paul, Omaha and Kansas City. There were millions of dollars' worth of equipment in my charge and, furthermore, mine was the controlling voice when we bought new engines, cars, coal and other things. Every one of the thousands of men in the mechanical department was a part of my responsibility too. That was quite a load for a young fellow who was just turning thirty-four; of course, they thought out there that I was thirty-eight at least. Sometimes they would think I was older. How strange it is that most of us pass through some of our years thinking that youth is a handicap.

I had learned a lot about picking men. I remember I got word that an old friend had left Arkansas City and was looking for a place. With a telegram, I arranged for him to come to Oelwein.

"Hello, Walt." There stood Gus Neubert, looking on me with as much pride and tenderness as if I had been his son. We embraced like a pair of Mexicans, slapped each other on the back. "Listen, Gus, you're master mechanic of this division. I need you."

Things had not been breaking right for Gus Neubert, and now, abruptly, everything became right again. Then I saw that Gus was having difficulty speaking, and I choked up too. We remembered those years when I had been, first a sweeper, and then an apprentice, and that Gus had been the one who fired me for horseplay in the shop, and that he took me back. I really needed Gus Neubert, though, and others like him. We had respect for each other because we shared the secrets of a mighty craft.

While running that job in Oelwein I was in close contact, for the first time in my life, with technical men who had learned what they knew about machinery in college. For one, there was Sam Stickney himself, son of the road's builder and president. Sam Stickney was general manager and vice-president. On his office wall up in St. Paul I used to see (and know the taste of envy) his diploma as a graduate of the Massachusetts Institute of Technology. In addition to Sam Stickney, there were other college-trained engineers and college mechanics in the railroad's high command. With all of these you had to hold your own.

This is significant: Some of those technically trained executives encountered frustration in their work simply because they were ineffective when they tried to interpret what they knew and what they wanted done to rough fellows in the shops. I had been pounding away at my correspondence courses for six or seven years, until there was no word or term of mechanical engineering used by those college men which lacked meaning when they spoke to me. I had inside of me the essence of their knowledge, and something more—I could get out on the floor of any shop, walk into any roundhouse and do any man's job, with calipers or hammer or with a turret lathe. I had not been handicapped by the overalled route that I had followed. I knew that with swelling satisfaction. I felt, when I tackled a tough job, that there was nothing I could not accomplish if I wanted to.

I had some troubling thoughts at Oelwein. Sometimes I felt that I had reached the end of the route along which my ambition had been driving me. In the railroad service they almost never promoted a motive-power man into the higher executive group, or so it seemed. At that time it seemed that a merchant, a lawyer or some financial man had a better chance of becoming a high railroad executive than any mechanic, no matter how profound his knowledge of the railroad. Oh, I knew that I could increase my understanding of the other departments by which a railroad serves the people, but I was restless and railroad pay was low. The work required me to deal every day with men in other lines who were receiving much more money for performing work involving less responsibility. This was apparent every time I talked with men who came to sell us locomotives, fuel,

miscellaneous supplies or the raw materials for the cars that
I was manufacturing in the shops. Of course, I was not very
far removed in time from situations in which the $350 I was
getting would have seemed a princely sum. Yet we now had
three children to be reared and educated—Thelma, Bernice,
and our new baby, Walter P. Chrysler, Jr. Like Bernice,
Walter Jr., was born there in Oelwein. Thelma first saw
the light of day in Salt Lake City.

The Stickneys were important figures in the Middle West.
The elder Stickney was a great and forceful character; to
please him, it was necessary to have a lot of drive and not
say "can't" when he said "can." There are many Stickney
legends, for he was a man who could not be bluffed by
anybody. Before that demon of statistics, Jim Hill, bought
the Burlington, so as to bring his Great Northern Line from
the Twin Cities down into Chicago, it looked as if there
might be a deal between them. One day Hill said to Stickney, "You've asked me several times to make the trip from
St. Paul to Chicago over your line. Next Tuesday, if you
like, let's make the run by daylight."

They left St. Paul in Stickney's private car, running
special, and when Mr. Hill had settled back in his chair,
forthwith he began to quote, from a little book in his vest
pocket, memoranda about his vast railroad system.

"Stickney, on the Iron Range division last month we
moved"—Mr. Hill mumbled through his whiskers as if he
did a sum in mental arithmetic—"let's see—three, four, and
carry one—yes, five, ten million tons of freight at five dollars
a thousand ton miles."

"That's nothing, Jim." Mr. Stickney had his pocket memorandum book up before his keen and handsome face. "Last
month, over our Omaha-Chicago division, we moved twelve
million tons at four dollars each thousand tons per mile."

"Stickney, you're lying!"

"Gosh, blink it, Jim, so are you."

Then they put away their books and watched the Mississippi Valley scenery rolling past their shrewd and understanding eyes.

Sometime thereafter the headquarters of the Chicago Great Western Railway were transferred from St. Paul to Chicago, and the heads of some of my friends among the high command had fallen, figuratively, in the basket. Whenever I went to see the boss in Chicago, I no longer found myself looking into the strong face of A. B. Stickney. The Stickneys were out; a new group had gained control. The new president was Samuel Morse Felton. After my first conversation with him, I said to myself, "From now on, life around here is going to be something."

Sam Felton was, they said, a railroad man of the old school. It would require a lot of space to list the railroads of which he had been the president and of which he was going to be the president. He had started his career in 1868, when he was fifteen; he became a rodman, then an engineer, a chief engineer, a general superintendent. Why, he had been president of the East Tennessee, Virginia & Georgia Railway when I had been just a sweeper in the Ellis shops. More than a score of railroads had been ruled by him before he ever laid eyes on me. Of course, I was still a young and sensitive man, but I made up my mind to work nineteen hours a day, if that should be necessary, to keep everything in flawless running order. I neglected no detail of my job. Almost constantly I was out on the line, riding in locomotive cabs, checking up, praising, blaming. Week after week, I would be away from home four or five nights out of seven, in my effort to keep the whole of our spread-out mechanism accurately reflected in my mind.

One night after a trip that had lasted a week, I got home at six o'clock, ate my supper quickly and then, dog tired, went to bed. It was nearly midnight when I was awakened. The telephone was ringing. The Oelwein dispatcher's voice said: "A wire from Mr. Felton. He wants you in Chicago tomorrow morning."

I rubbed my eyes and the back of my neck so as to become wide awake, pulled on my clothes, made sure I had my wallet, fat with annual passes over all important railroads, and left my sleeping family. I caught the next train, which arrived in Chicago early in the morning. It was 8:30 when I reached the president's office and was told by his secretary to go right in.

There was a foot-high stack of correspondence between the old man's arms, and his glasses were fixed half-way down his nose as he worked his way through the pile.

"Good morning, Mr. Felton."

He looked up at me, fiercely; then dropped his eyes and went on reading. He did not say a word. I stood erect in front of his desk for some minutes, and wrath was rising in me like a tide.

The Chicago morning papers were arranged neatly on a corner of the flat-topped desk which dominated that big throne room of the railroad. I took one of those papers, strode over to a chair near a window. I sat down, spread out the paper and put my feet on the wide window sill. I was boiling mad. I was not reading anything in the newspaper I clutched, but had time to read at least a column before Sam Felton barked at me: "What are you doing here, Chrysler?"

I got up. "Mr. Felton, I don't know. You sent me a telegram last night, asking me to be here this morning." He glared a full second.

"Oh, yes, oh, yes." He started through a lot of papers in a drawer, and when he raised up he was clutching in one hand, as if it were a piece of damning evidence, a train report. "Chrysler, how about this hot box on No. 2? We lost three minutes."

"Mr. Felton, I don't know."

"You don't know? You! The superintendent of motive power?"

"For a week I've been out over the division, inspecting the shops. I feel sure my chief clerk will have started an investigation on that delay." It was hard for me to hold a curb on my emotions, hard to be polite, but I pretty nearly managed it: "As soon as I can get a little time in my office, I'll make a full report on the matter."

"You ought to know now. I shouldn't have to ask for a report."

"Well, I don't know one so-and-so thing about it, for the reason I have given you: I've been traveling over the line for a week."

Then he started to moan and wail at me. I could feel the air going deeper and deeper into my lungs. Suddenly I plunged my hand into my inside pocket, and at the gesture Mr. Felton put his hands on the arms of his swivel chair and ceased to speak. What I pulled out was the symbol of my job and my authority—that wallet full of railroad passes. With a wide circle of my arm, I flung it down on his desk so hard that it bounced; and then I said —— Well, I was explicit.

Sam Felton never got a chance to close his mouth before I had stomped out of his office and slammed the door behind me. That is how I became an ex-railroad man.

I went from Felton's office on that December day directly to the flight of stairs with worn, white marble treads by which one descended to the basement bar of the Brevoort Hotel.

Possibly my recollection is faulty, but it seems to me that the mahogany bar was quadrangular in shape, and certainly all of my memories of the establishment are crowded with faces of old railroad friends. Anyway, that is where I went to lick my wounds, and in the middle of the morning, who should walk in but Bill Causey.

"What are you doing here so early, Walt?"

"What about yourself, Bill? You're supposed to be working."

"Come on, now; tell me all about it."

I told Causey all about the row, from its beginning down to my exit line as I left Felton's office. As the morning wore on, Causey revealed that his coming to the Brevoort was due to more than chance. Sam Felton, knowing we were friends, had sent him after me.

"Look, Walt; Felton's old enough to be your father. He doesn't want you to quit. You just happened to walk into him when he had a grouch."

"Well, he fixed the time for my call. I'm never going to give him the pleasure of firing me."

Other railroad friends arrived, and lacking any feeling of responsibility, I proceeded to enjoy myself while Causey, now and then, plucked at my arm or my lapel, urging me to say I'd remain at work. Bill stuck right by my side and we had our meals together there at the Brevoort. The night train for Oelwein left at 9:30, and as I headed through the station, Bill Causey was at my heels, still arguing with me to show some sense. The gateman stopped me just inside his barrier.

"Let's see your pass."

I had forgotten I had left my passes on Sam Felton's desk. I began to cuss, and Causey, for once that day, cut loose and laughed with real delight. He stood by, kidding me, while

116

I dug out of my pocket enough cash to pay for my ticket home to Oelwein. All the way across Illinois and into Iowa, through the night, Bill sat up with me, trying with friendly words to get me into a softer mood. I was glad of Bill's company anytime, anywhere, but I was in no frame of mind to go back to Felton.

I arrived home to find my wife stirring, getting little Thelma fed and off to school. I blurted out my news.

"What are you going to do, dad?"

"Get another job. I'll get a better one."

Well, if she was frightened by our plight, she never allowed me to suspect it; always, by the finest kind of understanding, of insight, she has known just how to handle me. If she had criticized then, if she had reminded me that I was up to my ears in debt, I might have flown off the handle. Instead, I got control of myself about as quickly as she filled my cup with coffee.

I went back to the office only to pack up my few personal belongings and to tell my chief clerk that I was moving out. Then I went home and began to monkey with my automobile. I fussed around the house for a day or two, and when I had my mind made up, I telegraphed to Waldo H. Marshall, the president of the American Locomotive Company, applying for a job.

The last time I had been in Marshall's company I had been buying locomotives. I had bought a lot of locomotives from him. He had been president of the American Locomotive Company for about three years at that time and we were on the best of terms. He knew me to be a lively, energetic fellow and had been so frank in his admiration that I turned to him naturally when I wanted a job. Building locomotives was the sort of work that I could do. Well, Marshall telegraphed back: "You must be kidding. Not possible you have left C. G. W." I convinced him after a further exchange of wires and letters. Marshall then invited me to go to Pittsburgh for a talk with James McNaughton, the company's vice-president in charge of sales. McNaughton was my kind of a man; he had been through all the grades of the railroad machinist's trade from apprentice to master mechanic and superintendent of motive power, and had then become general superintendent of the Brooks Works and Schenectady Works of the American Locomotive Company; he was in his fifties. He assured me, with great kindness, that I was coming to a place where I could make my talents count.

"You've got the type of background we need, Chrysler. We'll start you off as superintendent of the Allegheny shop." Superintendent? That had an impressive sound, but when I translated it, in terms of work, into a comparable job in railroad service, I realized that I had slipped down several notches: I was simply a foreman, and when I went to work I was wearing overalls. However, I was getting better wages than most foremen. They were paying me $275 a month.

The works manager of the Allegheny plant at that time was an elderly fellow who had the crusty look of a cold locomotive's fire box. If he had a sense of humor, I never detected it. He was tall, thin, and in those years he wore a flourishing mustache that bent downward from his hidden lip in a drooping shape that fixed on him a lugubrious expression.

The works manager had reason to feel sour then; he was being greatly troubled, and had been for months, by a new efficiency system. It was a method of scheduling the work, intended to give the firm a closer grip on costs, so that a job in one of the plants would cost just about the same as a similar job in another plant. I suppose this was intensely irritating to some of the old fellows who had been in the Allegheny plant for many years. The villain of the piece was an acquaintance of mine, a former superintendent of motive power on the Chicago Great Western Railway who had become a vice-president of the American Locomotive Company.

Well, I had rented a house, paying forty dollars a month to get one as good as we had lived in back in Oelwein. It was just a few days before Christmas when I went to the train and hugged my family in a reunion that put heart back into me. I had been mighty lonesome in the winter smoke of Pittsburgh. We were determined that we would have Christmas just as if our life had not been interrupted by a change. We managed to get our furniture delivered, and had it all unpacked and nicely stowed on Christmas Eve. The telephone had been installed and we were settled again. I did not have much cash, what with moving expenses, railroad fares and meeting the usual payment on my note at Van Vechten's bank. However, we had a small Christmas tree.

On Christmas morning, just when the children were squealing and giving other expressions of delight over their presents, the telephone rang. I stepped over a couple of dolls, a baby carriage and some blocks and picked up the receiver.

It was the works manager; he did not say "Merry Christmas."

"Chrysler?"

"Yes."

"Say, your friend, the efficiency expert in New York, no longer is vice-president. He got fired yesterday. Maybe you better go down to New York and see where you stand."

This fellow talking was the man I was expecting to go to

work for on the following morning. Wasn't that a Christmas greeting? There I was, a stranger coming to a new job in a town where I did not know my way around. I swallowed and with a wave of my hand tried to silence whoever was making flat notes come from a little toy trumpet. The works manager kept on talking, convincing me the efficiency expert had been fired. That did not trouble me in the slightest. I did not bother to explain to him that the president, Waldo Marshall, was my friend in the organization. What felt as if a cup of cold water had been thrown in my face was the revelation that the works manager did not want me around. Then he repeated himself:

"Yes, the thing to do, Chrysler, is to get on a train and run down to New York. Find out where you stand."

"Say, I've got a better idea. If you want to know where I stand, maybe you better get on the train and go down to New York and find out for yourself." Then I hung up on him and hoped that the crash would hurt his ear. I picked up the toy trumpet. It had three valves, and I did my best for a little while to play the tuba parts of the overture from William Tell.

Downhearted? Not me! I had all the confidence in the world. The next morning I put on my overalls and plunged into my work. Three months later I did not have a warmer friend than the works manager.

What was more important was the change in me. The fun I had experienced in making things as a boy was magnified a hundredfold when I began making things as a man. There is in manufacturing a creative joy that only poets are supposed to know. Some day I'd like to show a poet how it feels to design and build a railroad locomotive.

A succession of swift changes happened in our lives there in Pittsburgh. There had come to work for us the first servant we ever had, a girl, a little untrained foreigner. Mrs. Chrysler had needed help and we could afford, by then, to have a helper in our home—somebody who could clean up in the kitchen after Mrs. Chrysler cooked; somebody to clean the front porch and to do what now is called "laundry," but what was "washing" then; somebody to mind the three children in idle time. My wife, until that girl was hired, had been too heavily burdened. Incidentally, that same girl remained with us for two years after we moved to Michigan. When she did leave us, it was to go back to Pittsburgh to be married.

I got a new car in Pittsburgh, having been able to discharge my debt to Ralph Van Vechten's bank in Chicago, and so be free to make a deal for a Stevens-Duryea with a six-cylinder engine. On those Pittsburgh hills I felt the need for something new. I had become the works manager of the American Locomotive Company. This promotion had come to me in a little more than a year and a half after I abandoned railroading and took up manufacturing.

Almost from the start, I had been called assistant works manager, but until I knew my way around I rarely exercised the authority of the job—in overalls roving the plant for weeks, getting acquainted with a variety of activities housed in buildings that covered many acres. Along one side ran the Ohio River and close beside it was our iron foundry. Another huge building housed the truck shop. In another was the brass foundry and forge shop. Then there was that stimulating place, the erecting shop.

Our Allegheny plant began doing something it had not done during three preceding years; it began to make money. Every locomotive is a special job, tailored to suit the customer. We had reached a point where we were completing many new engines in our erecting shop. Each one, of course, had been sold before it was built. Orders for millions of dollars' worth of new locomotives came in—some of those orders coming in the Duquesne Club, from talking with men like myself who had started out as machine-shop apprentices, in overalls. In a machine age, can there be a better way to start?

David Francis Crawford would telephone me, "Chrysler, come over to the club and have lunch with me. I want to talk about locomotives." He was the general superintendent of motive power of the Pennsylvania Railroad Lines west of Pittsburgh; he had begun as an apprentice in the shops at Altoona. Throughout our meal together we would talk shop, getting our minds to meet on the specifications for a new series of locomotives. We were building all kinds of engines then; some were for the New York Central Lines, for service way over in our Schenectady plant's territory. One of the best customers was Loren H. Turner, superintendent of motive power of the Pittsburgh & Lake Erie Railway. One day Mr. Turner, while we talked at lunch, gave us an order for twenty-five new engines:

"Listen, Chrysler; I want to haul twelve Pullman cars on a one per cent grade at sixty miles per hour. I am going to buy twenty-five locomotives that can do that kind of work. Now you go back to the works and calculate your bid."

"Standard accessories? Injectors, lubricators ——"

"Yes, standard accessories, but these locomotives must be able to haul twelve Pullman cars on a one per cent grade at sixty miles per hour. Remember that!"

Those were the only specifications we had, except weight. Ours was the winning bid. My recollection is that the order totaled about $1,250,000; it would have cost twice as much to duplicate that order long before those engines were scrapped. We got one other big order from Mr. Turner, given to me while we devoured a rare steak the size of my forearm.

"Chrysler, I hear you're leaving."

"Going out to Flint, Michigan. We are expecting another baby in my family. I won't go till then."

"Then you'll have time to make some engines for me. It's no deal though, unless you agree to stay long enough to put these engines through your shop. That understood?"

"Oh, sure."

"Well, I want twenty-five switching engines."

"You'll get 'em, even if we have to work on Christmas."

Going out to Flint was the result of a telegram from a man whose name meant little to me when I read it at the bottom of his message: "James J. Storrow." He was inviting me to call on him in New York.

"Who is Storrow?" I asked a banker acquaintance at the DuQuesne Club.

"Oh, nobody; just the head of Lee, Higginson and Company. Then, too, you will find that he is a director of the company you work for."

"Well, if he wants to see me, I suppose I should go."

"You better had," the banker said.

"The message said he wanted to discuss an important matter."

"Chrysler, anything that Storrow wants to talk about to you will be important. How does it happen you were unaware that he is a director of American Locomotive?"

"The only ones I have to think about are Waldo Marshall and Jim McNaughton; they're my friends."

No. 43 Exchange Place was the New York address of Lee, Higginson and Company in 1911. I found it, not without difficulties, because I never had been in New York before that day. In my mind's eye I was still seeing fascinating visions of the fantastically high buildings when I was ushered into Mr. Storrow's office. He got up to greet me, saying, "So you're the fellow who transformed our Allegheny plant from a losing venture into a paying one?" Of course, it was not me; the best thing I had done in Pittsburgh had been to find the right kind of men for the right jobs. Actually, I had hired back a lot of good ones who had been fired before I came. But Mr. Storrow had not invited me down there to discuss the affairs of the American Locomotive Company. He wanted to know if I had given any thought to automobile manufacturing.

"Yes, sir. I've been thinking about it, off and on, for about five years."

"Well, then, if you are interested, I believe it could be arranged for you to go to work for the Buick Motor Company, of Flint, Michigan. It is the most important of the group of companies that make up General Motors. You know, I am now the chairman of the finance committee. For a few months last winter I was president of General Motors. The job I'd like to see you have is that of works manager for the Buick Motor Company."

"Sounds good to me."

"The president of Buick is a Flint man of sterling character. He has earned a great reputation as a carriage manufacturer, and we are all agreed that he is precisely the man to steer the company now. However, the automobile business is still new to him and he agrees with me that he needs someone with a lot of machinery experience to run the works."

I nodded and tried to keep from looking too happy.

"A great future in automobiles. That's my opinion as a banker."

"That's the way I feel about it too. I'm a transportation man, you see, and this is individual transportation ——" I shut up then, afraid to talk when I was feeling so much excitement.

"Would you be willing to meet Mr. Nash in Pittsburgh?"

"Be glad to."

"Well, I'll arrange that, and he'll probably invite you to look over the Buick plant. Remember, he is high-strung and ——"

"Yes?"

'Just a word of advice: This is a great opportunity for the right man."

About a week after I returned to Pittsburgh from New York, I got a telegram from Charles W. Nash, of Flint, Michigan. He named an early date when he was going to be in Pittsburgh, and asked if I would have lunch with him. I wired acceptance. Not many days thereafter I was shaking hands with him for the first time in my office at the works. We went to the Fort Pitt Hotel for lunch.

I suppose Charley was sizing me up during that meal; I know he did not tell me much; we seemed not to be the same breed of cats. Oh, we were cordial enough but the ice really wasn't broken until we had finished.

"Want a cigar, Chrysler?"

"Yes, I smoke panetelas."

As I said this, his dark mustache widened in a grin of appreciation. "You smoke panetelas? That's funny. I smoke them myself." In the time we smoked those slender brown rods down to butts we got better acquainted, and Nash asked me to visit his plant, the Buick Motor Company, at Flint.

McNaughton tried to talk me out of going. I was getting $8000 a year by then, and he fixed it so that my salary became $12,000. One thousand dollars every month! My wife and I were entranced at the bare thought of getting a raise that amounted almost to as much as my best railroad salary, that which I had been receiving when I quit the Chicago Great Western. Nevertheless, curious and eager, I kept my date with Nash at the Buick Motor Company works.

I was not with Charley five minutes after we shook hands. "I'll give you a pass," he said. "Takes you every place. Look around until tomorrow afternoon. Come in right after lunch and we'll sit down and talk things over."

I went to the little hotel to which he had directed me, put my bag in a room Nash had arranged for, and then went back to explore the automobile plant.

What I saw astonished me. Of course I was a machinist, and I was looking at workmen trained to handle wood. The bodies were being made of wood. In a big carpenter shop, long wide poplar boards were being bent and shaped in steam kilns. With wood they were admirably skillful, for most of them had been carriage builders, but wherever they were handling metal it seemed to me there was opportunity for big improvement. I saw a hundred such opportunities, so that I became excitedly eager, saying to myself, "What a job I could do here, if I were boss!"

Charley Nash fixed his eyes on me the instant I walked into his office. "What do you think?"

"Mr. Nash, I'd like to come here. I think I could be a useful man in this plant. I'm anxious to get into this business and with this company."

"Well, you've formed your opinion very quickly."

"I saw enough to be able to make up my mind."

"For instance, what?"

"Men were painting the chassis of each car as they would paint the panels of a carriage. I drive a car, and I know that by the time you get a new car home, all the under part of the chassis is splashed with mud; thereafter no one ever sees it."

Finally he said: "What salary do you want, Mr. Chrysler?"

"I've just had a raise, Mr. Nash. Over in Pittsburgh, when I told Mr. McNaughton that I was going to look at another job—well, they raised me from $8000 to $12,000 a year."

I could see immediately that Charley Nash was getting ready to focus his attention on something else. His interest in me was gone; he just seemed to collapse, the way a tire does when its air is let out.

"In this business we don't pay such salaries." He was shaking his head from side to side. He was not bargaining; he was simply winding up an incident in his day. There was reason for that: $12,000 really was a big figure in Flint in 1911. He did not know me; I was an outsider. But I was not prepared to let this chance get away from me.

"Mr. Nash, what will you pay?"

He thought awhile and pursed his lips. He scratched his head. Underneath his hair, Mr. Nash was doing sums with pieces of my life. If I was getting $12,000, surely I would be expecting a larger sum to tempt me from a job with people who liked me. Suddenly he sat up straight and spoke.

"Mr. Chrysler, we can't afford to pay over $6000."

"I accept it, Mr. Nash." He looked bewildered. Before I had been with him three months we were the best, the warmest kind of friends. We became friends, in fact, for life. Charley is a grand man.

·VI·

CONFLICTS IN A NEW CAREER

1912

"Full Authority Is What I Want"

· VI ·
CONFLICTS IN A NEW
CAREER

JACK CHRYSLER, our fourth and youngest child, was born in Pittsburgh. Although I was wild with eagerness to get to Michigan I stayed on here until I was sure my wife and this young son were getting along well.

When I was not excited by my prospects I was sad. After all, until then I had devoted my whole life to locomotives, and I loved them. They are noble mechanisms! Whenever I realized that the decision to go with the Buick Company would part me, forever probably, from association with railroad engines and railroad men as my companions, I was afflicted by regrets. Aside from these feelings I had to stop and think that I was taking my wife and children away from the comfort and dignity of the best situation I had ever achieved into a young and somewhat raw industry. But the new chance was exciting; it excited me as pioneering chances always have excited my ancestors, causing them to cross the ocean to an unformed America, to move northward into Canada, and then to go westward to the Kansas plains. I felt that same kind of thrill when setting out for Flint.

Certainly my entrance into the field of automobile manufacturing was happily timed. In that year, down in Dayton, Charles F. Kettering put the first self-starter on a Cadillac and shipped it to Henry M. Leland in Detroit; electrical starting, lighting and ignition fired the imagination of everybody in the industry; thereafter women might drive as easily as men. From that time on, everything splendid that had been predicted for automobiles began to come true.

Yet most automobiles were costing too much money. I soon began to find out why; the industry had grown up in a series of booms. Money was being spent recklessly by some; it was being wasted by others simply because they did not know how to curb waste. The great pressure on almost everyone in the business was time. If a company wanted a new plant of any kind, someone with authority was pretty sure to ask that the plant be produced quickly.

Right after entering the Buick plant as works manager, I asked for the piecework schedule. The clerk I asked looked at me blankly.

"The piecework schedule. These men out in the plant are being paid on a piecework basis. Where's the schedule?" There was some fluttering when my voice rose, but none around could produce such a schedule. There was no such record in the office that could be found. So I hustled out of the office building and went to the stamping plant.

My assistant over there, with whom I was just getting acquainted, was quite obliging. "Will you come in your office," I said to him, "so I can see your piecework record?" There were probably three or four thousand men working for Buick then; the stamping plant was filled with machines and men.

"Oh, the piecework record! Sure! I've got it right here in my pocket." He pulled out a little sheet of paper and unfolded it, so I could see the writing on it. There was nothing on that record about which kind words could be said; it simply was not a record of what I wished to know. In the

Allegheny works of the American Locomotive, we had to bid $40,000 or so on a locomotive job; bidding low enough to get the job and still make a profit. The only way we could do that was to know to a penny what it was costing us to drill a hole and what it cost to make an obscure little casting. All our locomotive work had been scheduled, and that was never simple. We used a slide rule to find a sound basis for our estimates; we felt we had to know precisely when the patternmakers would be through, how many days it would take to cast a cylinder, when the boilermakers, tankmakers, molders, machinists, and the other workmen, group by group, would be ready to pass along what they had made. In that way, thanks to painstaking study of every detail of all operations, we could promise to complete a locomotive on a certain day and keep our promise; moreover, we had been able to bid low and still give the company its profit. Even before working in Pittsburgh, we had been compelled to watch costs to the penny. In the railroad shops we had to know the cost of raw materials and how much labor would be required before we began to build a locomotive.

But in Flint we were making automobiles, not just one or two, but many every day. So from that time forward we had a piecework schedule at Buick—one that meant something.

Among the many good men at the Buick plant was a fellow named Chet Smith. He became my production manager. One day, about two weeks later, we stood together watching operations in a room where chassis after chassis was taking shape. In that time Buick was turning out about forty-five cars a day. Henry Ford was making hundreds of cars a day; in the next year—1913—his production reached 1000 cars a day.

This Buick chassis room was in a large brick building; it

must have been 70 feet wide and about 600 feet long. The roof was supported on wooden posts; there was a forest of these; they were nowhere more than twenty feet apart. In long rows were structures the height of a workbench. On these the chassis of each new Buick would be put together Four men would come up with members of a frame and rivet it together. Then other men would bring the axles and fix them on; others would hang the springs. Then the gang of workmen would go to another table and resume; painters would go to work on the chassis. After the sandpapering, the frames were painted; but it was a primary coat, rich with putty. This coat of paint would not dry in less than twelve hours. Next day they would sandpaper the frame a second time, and then paint it with a coat of liquid primary. After drying twelve hours the frame would get another light sandpapering, after which it received a finishing coat of varnish to make it shiny; that meant twelve hours more of drying. All those workmen had learned their painting trade in carriage factories. Well, it was such matters that Storrow and Charley Nash expected to have handled.

"Chet, this is all wrong. We've got to get each chassis out of here in two days instead of four."

"We can build a lot more cars if we do that."

"Of course. We can double our capacity, and we'll need more buildings and a lot more men."

We cut out the sandpapering and the glazing coat, which was treating metal as if it were wood. When someone would undertake to argue the point, the answer was:

"Listen, what is the use of finishing up the hidden parts of a chassis as if you were going to put it in a parlor? This stuff is caked with road mud on the first day it is used." Of course there were few highways outside the cities then, just country roads.

That change saved two days in building a chassis, and for a while we were kept busy bringing the rest of the plant production up to meet this change. But we had barely started; inside of six months we were at those chassis operations again. By running the temperature somewhat higher, we succeeded in drying two coats of paint in just half a day. Well, that is how Buick began to improve its factory performance, cut costs. Every minute of my time we were figuring out further ways to adapt carriage-craft operations to automobile building. With just those changes in operation we succeeded in improving production from forty-five cars a day to seventy-five, practically in the same space and with a most impressive saving. We knew we could do better, though, if we just kept on hunting out all kinds of waste.

Right in that same room where each Buick chassis was being made, we evolved a better working method merely by supporting the roof on stouter trusses and taking out the posts that were in every workman's way. Perhaps it was a year later that we made another outstanding improvement. Instead of having the whole room filled with tables where frame members were riveted and where other operations proceeded until, one by one, each table supported a finished chassis, we had the vast room empty of all but four or five tables supported on stanchions, with benches close at hand.

Beyond these, extending clear to the far end of the room, was a trough, a pair of tracks made of two-by-fours. When a chassis was complete with axles, springs and wheels, a little chain hoist was used to lift it off the table to the floor, astride the track; then it was pushed along from hand to hand; two men put the fenders on, others in turn added a gas tank, and finally the chassis got its body. Once we started making cars that way we had the whole scheme of mass production going, although it was some years before people said "mass production." We were just doing it without bothering about terms.

We were doing our painting before we started to assemble; in that way we could have a stock of parts painted and ready without holding other workmen. Then we developed a way to squirt paint, using air pressure; it was the old principle of the atomizer. We went on and on with one improvement after another until, in that same room, instead of merely forty-five cars we were making 200 cars each day.

Henry Ford, after we developed our line, went to work and figured out a chain conveyor; his was the first. Thereafter we all used them. Instead of pushing the cars along the line by hand, they rode on an endless-chain conveyor operated by a motor.

Nowadays, when you go into an automobile factory, you see a lot of parts almost effortlessly put together and so smoothly that in about fifteen minutes what was just a naked frame when you began to watch has become an automobile full of gas and oil, being driven off under its own power. Compare that with the four days that it used to take to assemble a chassis. Better still, call up a vision of the most costly automobiles of 1912; then take a ride in any one of the least expensive of the 1937 models. Believe me, it has been a thrilling quarter of a century for those of us who have been making automobiles, who have had our hands and brains involved with the details of this industrial triumph.

In my first years with Buick, there was a chance for sharp improvement in production any time we came upon a workman who was waiting for materials.

"What's the matter here, my friend?"

"These crankshafts aren't coming along fast enough. Spend half my time waiting." That would be the cue. When you had figured out a way to speed the crankshaft flow, some other kink would be revealed. Starting with the assembly line, we worked backward through the plant until everything was tied in. Every new thing was an invention. As soon as one problem was revealed and straightened out, twenty other problems had arisen. The motors began to get their shapes riding on a conveyor line; then the axles, crankshafts, cam-shafts; until now it would be difficult to find an operation which requires men to exert their muscles like they used to. The workmen have machines to do their bidding.

Out of our insistent needs, machine tools were developed. A machine-tool salesman would no more than show his head inside my office than we'd be after him: "We have to have a machine that can ——" Then he'd take his pencil out and write down what we needed; back in his home factory he would feed the problem to the engineers: "How can we do thus and so?" They would work it out, sometimes swiftly, sometimes not for months or even years. We kept on reaching out for better ways, for better things, until evolutionary changes were occurring in the steel industry, in the machine-tool trade, in the cotton fields down South, everywhere raw materials came from. We were insistent—imperiously some-times. We were making the first machine of considerable size in the history of the world for which every human being was a potential customer.

Charley Nash was precisely the man needed to guide General Motors through the condition in which he found it when he left the Durant-Dort Carriage Company in Flint to be-come the president of Buick; he was greatly admired in the town, and William C. Durant had wisely recommended him to James J. Storrow. Storrow spoke for the investment group. Nash may have known little about automobiles when he began in 1910, but he did know how to handle men; he knew how to run a factory. Above all, he was loyal; you could not hope to find a man more honest. He never was the sort of fellow to become reckless with anybody's money. Sometimes when he turned his thumbs down on some expenditure for the Buick plant, would not let me buy some new machines we wanted, I'd tell him he was tighter than a barrel without a bung. "Charley," I'd say imploringly, in the manner of a little boy, "please show me the first nickel you ever earned. Mr. Storrow says you've got it hidden somewhere."

Nash had gone with Durant when Billy started in the carriage business about 1886 or '87. Charley had been bound out as a boy to a Michigan farmer; then he went into Flint and got a job with Whiting & Richardson, a hardware firm. He was a handy fellow to have around, because he had a knack for setting up agricultural machinery; they had a big farmer trade there. He was such a hard worker that Billy Durant was impressed by him.

"How would you like to come over to the factory, Nash?"

Charley said he thought he'd like it: Durant gave him a wage of $1.25 a day, and set him to work in the blacksmith shop. He had been there only a few days when he approached Durant.

"Say, Mr. Durant, I've been pounding iron for Mr. McCruttin, the blacksmith, but I'm wasting time. You can get a little power hammer there. Wouldn't cost more than thirty-five dollars, and it would do more pounding in a day than I can do in a month."

Billy bought the hammer and put Charley at another job. Next time he saw him he was working at a drill press on cart braces, but he had rigged up his drill press with an overhead spring and brought it into action with a foot pedal, so as to keep both hands free. Young Nash was handling about five times as many cart braces as his predecessor at that drill press.

"Charley," said Durant, "we'll get another man here. You

see if you can't straighten out the trimming shop for me."

There Charley quickly diagnosed the trouble. "Your purchasing agent is buying cheap tacks; they are roughly made and cut the men's mouths. Besides, they are much too small; the men drop more on the floor than are used."

Charley Nash had a real talent for manufacturing and he moved right on up until he was the production manager of the big carriage business that Durant and his friend, J. Dallas Dort, had built up from next to nothing until they were producing 150,000 vehicles a year. When Charley Nash went to work for Buick, though, and then became president of General Motors, he was working for General Motors and not for Billy Durant. They did not see eye to eye. Nash and Storrow had points of view more nearly in focus. However, Billy Durant did not enter my life until a few years later.

When I had served three years as works manager at Buick, Charley Nash was still paying me the same salary at which I had started with the company. In that boom town of Flint, I was almost conspicuous because I got relatively so little; or, so it seemed.

Executives out there sat in swivel chairs between a roll-top desk and a big flat-topped table. One day I walked into Nash's office and rested my knuckles on his table.

"Charley, I want $25,000 a year."

"Walter!" It was pretty nearly a scream, the way he uttered my name.

"Now, Charley, we've gotten along fine. We are making good. Here in Buick, we've got the one company that has been making money."

"Walter ——"

"Just a minute until I have finished. I've waited a long time before saying this. When I came here I was getting $12,000; I took this job for $6000, and you haven't given me a raise. I want $25,000 a year, or I'm going to leave you."

"Walter, this is something I'll have to talk about with Mr. Storrow." I walked out, smoking one of my own panetelas.

In a couple of days I learned that Storrow had arrived in town. Nash and Storrow were in conference. Then word was brought that they would like to see me down in Charley's office.

"What's this all about, Walter?"

"Not much to it. You know how I came here. You know I was getting $12,000, and now I'm getting $6000; after three years of the hardest — I want $25,000 a year. By —"

"Don't get excited, Walter." Mr. Storrow did everything but pat me like a pet horse. "Don't get excited; you're going to get your $25,000."

"Yes? Well, thank you; and by the way: Next year I want $50,000." I was forty years old. When I got home, I really started to enjoy that raise. I told my wife.

"Dad! I knew you'd do it!"

Those words contained everything I wanted to hear. In all our life together, there never has been a time when she was putting the slightest pressure on me to change my ways. She's never nagged me, never thrown anything up to me; yet I am quite aware that I have made countless decisions after calculations in which the decisive factor has been my knowledge of what my wife would regard as becoming and proper. It was about the time I got that raise that we discussed an evening gown. She had denied herself a lot, I knew.

"Aw, get two," I said. But she shook her head. If our feet remained on the ground—and I know they did—my wife should get seventy per cent of the credit.

That year, 1915, when I began to draw an annual salary of $25,000, was eventful for General Motors. I used some of my salary to buy company stock, but I could not get as much as I liked, because the price was rising swiftly. The Buick factory had become something to make any man who worked there proud. However, although none of us knew it, the gentleman who had made Buick a great name, who had put General Motors together, was coming back; that was Durant, a genius—William C. Durant. His triumph was to be compared with Napoleon's return from Elba, only this time Napoleon was to win for much longer than 100 days.

When I was still playing Indians and shooting marbles out in Kansas, a boy of ten or eleven, Durant was a young insurance man of Flint. He has told me that the business was paying him about $900 a year when he saw a chance to become a manufacturer. He borrowed $2000 with which to start, bought the patents and other existing rights of a road-cart company for $1500, and promptly sold a half interest to J. Dallas Dort, a friend of his, for $1000. Before he was forty, Billy Durant was a millionaire; one who felt that he had barely started. This is not the place to tell what bitter circumstances caused him to lose control of General Motors and his hand-reared pet, Buick; but having lost, he proceeded to form another company, Chevrolet. The first Chevrolet was made in April, 1913; two years later, Billy Durant was proceeding toward successful conclusion of a scheme whereby control of the giant General Motors would be regained for him by his comparatively little Chevrolet Company. Of course, Durant had a vast block of General Motors stock to begin with; he had kept his original holdings; members of his family, business associates, old friends and others who had faith in his genius, had kept their stock. Some day, they felt, Billy would get back on top. In 1912, a year before the first Chevrolet was sold, his plan began maturing.

Three years later, on September 16, 1915, Billy Durant walked into the General Motors stockholders' meeting.

Quickly and quietly he asserted and established that he, the founder, was once more in control; that is, Chevrolet controlled General Motors, and Durant, with the Du Ponts, controlled Chevrolet. As Chevrolet was not a suitable embracing name, an exchange was made and the captor took its captive's title. A division was set up inside the magic circle so that besides Buick, Cadillac and all the others there was a new division henceforth to be known as Chevrolet. Durant had spent $27,000,000 of Du Pont money to accomplish this end.

Mr. Storrow had retired from the board in the preceding June; his place as chairman of the finance committee was taken by Louis K. Kaufman, of the Chatham and Phoenix Bank, of New York. Mr. Kaufman had given tremendous aid to Billy Durant in his fight. I remember seeing him for the first time, not long afterward, walking through the Buick plant. Our friendship which began then, has continued ever since. He has served through all these years on the General Motors board.

Meanwhile Nash and Storrow were persuaded we three ought to work together in something else. I was willing, provided we could make our plan work. We wanted to buy out the Packard Motor Car Company; plants, agencies, everything. Mr. Storrow was coming out to Detroit to make the trade. The negotiations had proceeded so smoothly until then that we counted on it as practically settled. Mr. Nash had resigned as president of General Motors as of June 1, 1916. I was general manager of Buick.

One day, who should walk into my office but William C. Durant; he was taking over Nash's job as president of General Motors. He got right down to business.

"Mr. Chrysler, I'd like to hire you as president of the Buick Motor Company."

"I want to be perfectly frank with you, Mr. Durant. If a plan on which I am negotiating now goes through, I'm quitting here."

"This is a great company. You've been doing a splendid job."

"If this plan goes through, Mr. Durant, I'm committed."

Billy nodded, smiling with understanding. "How long will it take you to learn for sure?"

"Thirty days, I think."

"I'll be in Flint for thirty days. When you make up your mind, you call me. I'd like to talk to you."

I cannot hope to find words to express the charm of the man. He has the most winning personality of anyone I've ever known. He could coax a bird right down out of a tree, I think. I remember the first time my wife and I entered his home. The walls were hung with magnificent tapestries. I had never experienced luxury to compare with Billy Durant's house. In five minutes he had me feeling as if I owned the place.

The Packard plan blew up. However, by that time Charley Nash had found something else, the old Jeffery plant out in Kenosha, Wisconsin. It could be bought, Mr. Storrow told me, for less than $5,000,000. Charley was hot for it, and Mr. Storrow too. A couple of other General Motors men, W. H. Alford and C. B. Warren, were joining, and Mr. Storrow, in urging me, said, "You will be one of the principal owners and partners, getting satisfaction out of working for your own company." Even though this enterprise was beginning as a small company, it had a tempting sound. One drawback was that the Chryslers would have to become strangers in still another town, and we had been strangers in a lot of places. For the first time in our life together, my wife and I were really settled down. Finally, for that reason, I telegraphed Mr. Storrow that I had decided not to join. That was a wrench, because I thought the world of Nash and Storrow. Then Mr. Storrow wrote me:

Dear Walter: . . . You have my very best wishes in whatever you undertake and you may rely upon our cordial cooperation to the utmost possible extent at any time that we can be of assistance to you. I am inclosing a circular showing how we are offering the stock of the Nash Motors Company, simply to let you know what we are up to. . . . Let me know sometime when you are coming to New York, and if I am in Boston, I shall be very glad to run over and see you. . . . I do not want to let our friendship drop, and ask you to co-operate to see that it doesn't.

It never did; until the day of his death, James Storrow was one of my best friends.

The resignation of Charley Nash left a big hole in the General Motors organization. He had been a vital factor in the success of the corporation and I hated to see him go away. Not only was he a loyal friend and a grand man but I knew him to be one of the country's greatest industrialists. The tremendous success that he has made at Racine with the Nash Motors Company is something any of the friends he left behind him at General Motors would have predicted from the day he left Michigan to go to Wisconsin.

Soon after I had made my decision, I telephoned Durant. He asked, "When do you want to see me?"

"Seven o'clock in the morning." I went to work early because it was my habit to walk through the factories and get to my desk before the offices opened. Seven o'clock found Billy Durant right on my doorstep.

I dropped into my swivel chair between my roll-top desk and my wide table; Durant seated himself on the opposite side of the table. I was going to ask him for a raise.

"I'll pay you $500,000 a year to stay on here as president of Buick." He just sprang it on me that way; he did not bat an eye. I couldn't think for a few seconds.

"Mr. Durant, the salary you offer is, of course, far and away beyond anything I expected, but ——"

"Now, Walter" (we were getting well acquainted fast), "you just put aside, for the time being, all your plans of getting into business for yourself. I don't blame you for the ambition, but I ask you to give me just three years of yourself."

"There's one thing ——"

"You shouldn't run away from this proposition, Walter. Nash is going. But the boys here stood by you, and now ——"

"They have stood by me, as you say, but I'm standing by them when I say that I can accept only if I'm to have full authority. With their help, I can run this property. I don't want interference. I don't want any other boss but you. If you feel that anything is going wrong, if you don't like some action of mine, you come to me; don't go to anybody else and don't try to split up my authority. Just have one channel between Flint and Detroit: from me to you. Full authority is what I want."

He was beaming at me then. I saw him touch his fingers lightly to the table top for emphasis. "It's a deal," he said.

When we got our deal worked out on paper, it was even better than the offer that had overwhelmed me in the office; he arranged for me to draw $10,000 cash a month, and at the end of each year of the three for which I contracted to work for General Motors, I had the right to take the rest in cash or else to claim its equivalent in stock at the price as of the day we signed the contract. Of course, I always took the stock.

Billy was a forceful character, so, I suppose, collisions were inevitable. One day when I had been president of Buick about three months we were working out some new arrangement about our branches; Buick had sixteen branch houses then, one in St. Louis, one in Kansas City, one in New York, one in Chicago, others at scattered points; but one of the best was in Detroit. Each one of them was earning for the company about $200,000 a year; a nice business.

Well, it was then I had a visitor, Richard Collins, our former sales manager—"Trainload" Collins.

He had quit Buick and moved over to Detroit; I suppose he did this so as to be near Durant. That was a natural move, since he was one of Durant's close associates.

"What's on your mind, Dick? This is my rush day."

"Walt, I just drove over from Detroit in my car to tell you I've bought the Detroit Buick branch from Durant."

"Oh, no, you haven't. I'm president of Buick."

"Oh, yes, I have." It seemed to me that he mocked my tone a little. "That's why I came over. Want to talk to you about it."

"Listen, Dick; you can't talk to me about it. Even if Durant is president of General Motors, I'm running the Buick Motor Company. Don't you think I'm not." By that time I had put my coat on, cracked my derby hat down on my head and was at the door.

"But, Walt, I've made the deal."

"You haven't made any deal. You might as well go downstairs and get in your otherwise-than-Buick automobile and drive on back to tell Durant that you have not bought the Detroit branch. I'm going to be there about as quick as you are, because I'm going right now."

That same afternoon I walked into Billy's office.

"I don't want to take up too much of your time, but have

you forgotten the contract I've got with you to run the Buick Motor Company?"

"Certainly not. What's happened?"

"Dick Collins came to Flint and told me he had bought the Detroit branch. If he has, I'm through."

"Now, Walt, don't get excited. You know Dick Collins! He's been after me for months about that branch. He coaxed and urged ——"

"As long as I'm the president of Buick, I'm going to run it. If there is any policy you wish to change, policies that concern all the companies, Cadillac, Oldsmobile, Buick, Chevrolet, and the others, just tell me, and I'll carry out your orders. But don't interfere with the Buick organization. I'm responsible for Buick unless you've changed your mind about me; if you have, you've got my resignation now."

"Now, Walt, Dick Collins hasn't bought any Buick branch."

"He says he has."

"You leave that to me."

"All right. Give me a memorandum stating that you have not sold the Detroit branch." He called in his stenographer, dictated what I had asked for, and I went back to Flint, feeling better. I think it was a year at least before we had another difference of opinion.

One day my drop-forge superintendent came to tell me, "Mr. Durant wants me to move over to Detroit and run a drop-forge plant for General Motors." We were paying him $8000.

"Do you want to move away from Flint?" I asked.

"No, but Mr. Durant is going to pay me $12,000."

"You better go, then," I said.

As soon as I could get hold of Billy I asked, "If you want some man from here, tell me and I'll help you get him. But

147

don't go into the plant over my head and interfere with my men, unless you want me to quit." Billy just could not help doing that sort of thing. If he saw a man he wanted, he waved a wand of gold. He offered to cancel the arrangement; of course that could not be done. It would not be fair to the man. So I told him, "He's your man now, at $12,000."

A number of arguments on matters of that kind occurred during our three years together.

I remember I went to see him once and said, "Billy, for the love of —— please, now, say what your policies are for General Motors. I'll work on them; whatever they are, I'll work to make them effective. Leave the operations alone; the building, the buying, the selling and the men—leave them alone, but say what your policies are."

Billy laughed at me. "Walt, I believe in changing the policies just as often as my office door opens and closes."

I wagged my head and said, "You and I can never get along." That's the kind of fellow he was, though; we'd fight, and then he'd want to raise my salary. The automobile industry owes more to Durant than it has yet acknowledged. In some ways, he has been its greatest man.

I would think of Charley Nash and his warnings. Then I'd speak as gently as I knew how: "Billy, I'm getting all the money I want. Salary be damned! Will you please leave the Buick organization alone?"

·VII·

MEN, MOTORS, AND MY WIFE

1920

"I Will Go Back To Work"

· VII ·

MEN, MOTORS, AND MY WIFE

I KNOW Billy Durant believed that in Buick we had built a beautiful pattern of what an automobile-manufacturing company should be like. What disturbed him was that Buick was being built so strongly that it overshadowed everything else in General Motors; at least that was what he said. What had been accomplished with Buick, Billy said, was what he wanted to accomplish for Pontiac, Olds, Cadillac and the others. He wished each one to be complete. I felt that Buick ought to be allowed to do its very best. Sometimes we found ourselves in arguments; but also we had a lot of fun. When we saw something that we wanted, we could go, or send, and get, generally, just what we wanted. But sometimes it took more than money to get our way.

Down in Dayton there was a genius that we needed in Detroit. This was Charles F. Kettering, a brilliant inventor. Some time after he had made the first electric starter, Billy Durant had bought from him and his associate, Edward Andrew Deeds, their Dayton Engineering Laboratories Company, the "Delco."

When the trade was completed Billy Durant came to Flint and discussed it with Nash in my presence. This was before I had become president of Buick, while I was works manager. Billy explained that to get Delco it had been necessary to include in the purchase price some money for an air-cooled car which was being developed at Delco. There had been talk that this automobile might revolutionize the low-priced field. Turning to me, Durant said, "Now that we've got this air-cooled car, what would you do with it?"

"Throw it in the ash can." In those days I spoke bluntly by habit. I saw Billy Durant grin, and then he nodded in full agreement with my judgment. What I felt was that he had made an important purchase when he got Delco. The aim, of course, was to reduce the costs of the starting-lighting-ignition units. From the beginning of the automobile business high costs have been a challenge; that is the reason men do not have to be rich to possess an automobile. Few Americans are so poor they may not hope to own a car. Yet this is true only because the industry has struggled to be able to sell its wares cheaper and cheaper even as the cars became better and better. Their steady improvement, of course, has been the fruit of inventive minds like that of Kettering.

Becoming president of Buick, and first vice-president of General Motors, in charge of operations, I was eager to get Kettering to leave the management of Delco to someone else and come up to Detroit. Most of my associates said I would never be able to induce Ket to leave Dayton, to leave his pet business, his friends, his home, his farm, and move to Detroit. I knew you could never tempt him much with money. Charley really does not care a hang about money. But I sold him with the offer of an exciting job.

"You're the man to steer the whole engineering intelligence of General Motors," I said. What we were offering him was a chance to solve mechanical and scientific problems endlessly, and I could see his eyes glitter with desire. He took the job and thereafter General Motors began to get the full use of the most important thing acquired with Delco. In Kettering the company had a bargain.

In the development of the great modern business corporations as servants of mankind, men have devised a creative force that transcends themselves. None of these corporations are perfect yet, of course; but before you condemn their crudities remember how young they are and then ask yourself what other time in history can show anything to compare with these teams of men, in capacity to enrich mankind, in capacity to extend human powers in almost any direction we may wish to go.

Kettering has become a great scientist; then he was an inventor, and we wanted him because of his visions, because through him there probably would be revealed greater tasks for the force we represented.

Nourished by such a mind as that of Kettering of General Motors or Fred Zeder of the Chrysler Corporation, a great corporation's departmentalized intelligence becomes still greater; but to support a Kettering there must be other kinds of minds, those of production men, of merchants, of mechanics, of advertising men and countless others. When all these minds, through organization, are made to function as a single intelligence, each member of which is a special gifted part, why, then you can expect to produce magic. Nowhere in the world is there a people with wealth so widespread as in America; nowhere is there a people who have so much. It seems to me quite obvious that we do not owe this difference to a few outstanding men; we owe it to a scheme of working whereby a lot of varied intelligences in a great business organization pool their most effective parts.

At a time when I was impatient to talk with Billy Durant about war contracts, I got a train out of Detroit for New York and on the following morning went to his office.

I seemed to be in a room full of Napoleons at various stages of Napoleonic careers, and I decided to vanish from the scene.

I left Durant's office, caught a train to Washington, and went directly to the office of Col. Edward Deeds, who had been associated with Kettering in Delco and now was in charge of aircraft production for the War Department.

"Chrysler, we need that Buick plant. We've got to have airplane engines. I've been wondering when you were going to come down here and help us out."

"Well, here I am."

Within three hours I had an order for 3000 Liberty motors. I took rolls of blueprints back to Flint.

At the plant, my own offices were made into a drafting room and we started in on a twenty-four-hour schedule. We had cots brought to the offices and slept there until we lost track of time. I remember that we did not go home for two weeks. Deeds had said: "Some of these other manufacturers are three or four months ahead of Buick, but we are not getting the production we must have; deliveries are slow. Can you fellows do better?" He had meant this as a challenge, so I passed it on to the organization.

The plant had to be tooled for this new operation and the young fellow who was in charge of Buick tooling was the plant's master mechanic, K. T. Keller. Today he is President Keller, of the Chrysler Corporation.

I had liked Keller's looks the first time I had seen him, shortly after I had come from Pittsburgh to Flint to start my career as an automobile man. Keller a month or so before had gone to work for General Motors as a member of the central office staff, working most of his time on Cadillac. He was only twenty-seven then, but already he was an old hand in the automobile business. He had that same love for machines that had dominated my life, and a further bond between us was that he had served a special apprenticeship in the Westinghouse machine shop, erecting, designing and engineering. When he was only twenty-four he was assistant to the superintendent of the Westinghouse automobile engine department. Thereafter, deliberately, as a part of his own scheme of education he had worked at many jobs: chief inspector of a Detroit factory making automobile axles, foreman of the general machine shop of the Metzger Motor Car Company, with the Hudson Motor Company working on heavy repairs and chassis testing, and next as chief inspector of the Maxwell plant. Keller had lots of fire and his feet were on the ground; he was as stanch a fellow as you would want to see. He had left General Motors and had gone to Indianapolis, where he was working for the Cole Motor Car Company, when I succeeded in hiring him. He was less than thirty when he became master mechanic of Buick. He was a big factor in Buick's production of Liberty motors. When he was told to go ahead, a job was as good as done.

Thanks to Keller, it did not take long to make tools for the new operations; but there were other difficulties growing out of the fact that certain phases of the manufacturing were going on outside of Buick. For example, Ford had the contract to make all the cylinders for the Liberties. This meant that we could not produce engines any faster than we could get cylinders from Ford, and I was fearful that we would fail to get our requirements as swiftly as we needed them. Then I found out that Ford was having trouble making the overhead camshaft cylinder heads. We were making them easily. So I went to the Ford plant and made a trade with Harold Wills.

In those days Harold was an important figure in the Ford organization; today he is with Chrysler. Not only is he a thorough manufacturer, he is a great chemist and metallurgist. One of the latest benefits for our organization of his research is a new alloy called molo steel. But in that wartime hurry for production we had no thought of a future when we would be associated in a corporation then unborn.

"Wills," I said, "you can't make those cylinder heads and we can. Let's trade, cylinders for cylinder heads." I had some of our cylinder heads with me, finished, ready for assembly. Harold had to consult with Henry Ford and some Government official, but in about a week we were able to complete the trade and then, at Buick, we rushed into production. We had our first Liberty engine on test in two months after that trip to Washington.

Shortly after we began deliveries on that first order for 3000 twelve-cylinder Liberties we got another order for eight-cylinder airplane engines. By that time we were taking on all kinds of war work: trench helmets, hospital equipment, trucks, tanks and other things of metal. There was so much work, so many things to be done from day to day, there was hardly time to think.

It had been my intention to discuss those war contracts with Billy Durant, on that hurried visit to New York, but I had gone ahead without consulting him. He never took me, to task for that, however. He knew we were busy, and he had his own hands full to boot.

Once I had gone to New York in obedience to a call from him; he wished to see me about some matter. For several days in succession I waited at his office, but he was so busy he could not take the time to talk with me. It seemed to me he was trying to keep in communication with half the continent; eight or ten telephones were lined up on his desk. He was inhuman in his capacity for work. He had tremendous courage too. He might be risking everything he had, but he never faltered in his course. He was striving to make completely real his vision of a great corporation. Men, big men, came and went at his command. "Durant is buying" was a potent phrase in Wall Street then.

During a lull I gained his attention for a minute. "Hadn't I better return to Flint and work? I can come back here later."

"No, no. Stay right here." I waited four days before I went back to Flint; and to this day I do not know why Billy had required my presence in New York. Compared with what I had to worry me in Flint, I know that he had vastly greater worries.

For a month, or longer, we had been negotiating with a Milwaukee firm for the frames for Buick in the coming year. Little by little we were moving toward a deal; we were getting the price down. The Milwaukee plant was operating at about forty per cent of capacity; they wanted the business very much, and we were hoping to conclude a satisfactory trade by making the organization realize Buick would be in the market for frames in other years. This matter was what occupied my mind on a day when my secretary interrupted me to say it was time I attended the big booster luncheon of the chamber of commerce. As president of Buick, I would be expected to speak.

In those days, during the war and afterward, Flint was afflicted with a serious housing shortage. The prize that had lured thousands of strangers there was good wages, work. Near by me, Dallas Dort was talking; he was Durant's old partner in the carriage business, and long a resident of Flint. He was the president of the chamber of commerce.

"Boys!" he shouted, and waved a telegram above his head as if it were a banner. "I've got great news for you." When they became silent, he said, "Here's a wire from William C. Durant. He says he has just authorized the spending of

157

$6,000,000 to build a General Motors frame plant in Flint."

The businessmen of Flint went wild at that, and none could blame them. Most of the millions, they felt, would pass across their store counters over and over. Flint was booming! But I was feeling worse than sour. Had that telegram that Dort displayed been a red flag and myself a bull, I could have been no more enraged.

Then the toastmaster called on me for remarks. I suppose he expected them to be in keeping with the cheering.

I spoke to him from my seat. "I haven't anything to say—only this: not so long as I stay here will General Motors have a frame plant in Flint. Right now you lack facilities to house the men and women who have been attracted here by work. What sort of a mess will we be in if a bigger crowd is drawn into Flint?" Then I got up and left the luncheon.

The next day there was a board meeting of General Motors in Detroit, and Billy, smiling, brought up the subject of building a frame plant in Flint. I interrupted him.

"Why haven't you talked to me about this frame plant? That would be only fair."

I was far from tactful or polite, I suppose, but I was mad. My feelings had been hurt and my great responsibilities ignored.

"The corporation needs ——"

"How do you know this frame plant will cost $6,000,000?"

"Here's the estimate." He fluttered papers toward me; Billy could get mad too.

"Who made it?"

He named one of his cronies, a tireless worker.

"I'll bet you haven't got a layout for this six-million-dollar plant." Well, I confess freely that I have forgotten how Billy retorted to my challenges; undoubtedly, he felt that a frame plant was vital to his bigger plans.

I went on talking, "It would take two years to build a frame plant. Sure, it will be almost entirely automatic; but it will take three years to learn to run it. We can't recruit that kind of talent overnight. Mechanics of the kind required are not to be found around here. It will cost more in five years than we would pay for frames in ten years. We can go out right now and buy frames for General Motors for every car division, at a price that will save a million and a half a year."

Billy and I were having it hot and heavy when Jonathan Amory Haskell began saying things to cool us off:

"That's quite a statement, Walter. We ought to listen, because you are the production man at this table." Then he suggested to Durant that a committee including Raskob, Haskell and myself be appointed to investigate the frame situation, to see if a single purchase of frames would save as much money as I had said could be saved. Billy said, "All right."

We could yarn about that matter now and laugh, but at the time I realized Billy Durant would be no more able to forgive such an affront than an Indian. The way he saw it, I suppose, was that I had put myself athwart important plans of his. His head was filled with matters unrevealed and unfulfilled.

Then I sent for the head of the firm that was making our Buick frames and offered him a fabulous order, subject to a satisfactory price. We made a contract, which was approved, whereby his company was to supply frames for all makes of General Motors cars for a term of five years at a scale of prices sliding downward as quantities increased. As a result of that pooled buying, the corporation in the next year saved $1,750,-000 in comparison with the various prices we had paid for frames the year before. When the five-year term expired I understand that contract was renewed for five years more. However, within a few months after that dispute, my connection with General Motors ceased. Billy was nice to me after that, as nice as only Billy Durant knows how to be, but I felt—indeed, I knew—he could not forgive me for my heated opposition.

Durant and I had a couple of arguments in 1919. One, I remember, had to do with my report on a tractor plant in Janesville, Wisconsin. General Motors had been buying into the tractor business, and I had been delegated to go and see what had been bought. My judgment on the enterprise was not stated, I suppose, in tactful phrases.

"The Janesville Machine Company?" I echoed a question in our board meeting in the summer of 1919. "You've paid too much money for it. I know about the plant. I've been through it. I've seen the one-hundred-and-twenty-two-acre tract on which a new factory is being built. I don't like to see this company putting part of its strength into the tractor business, because it takes so long to get your money out. You've got to give three and even five years' time. Leave that kind of business to the corporations that are geared to it."

Eventually, the company suffered heavy losses in the tractor business. But at that time there were many other items in the spending program that I did not like. Billy Durant says that he did not like some of them, either, but at the time I was arguing with Billy.

"What am I roaring about? I'm roaring as a stockholder, if you really want to know. Everything I have in the world is in this company. I don't want to lose it."

After the meeting Mr. Haskell came to see me. "You just flew off the handle today; we all do that. So did Billy. He wants you to forget it."

"O.K."

"You'll come back tomorrow? We want to finish the meeting."

"Yes, I'll come."

All those people were my friends; we still are friends; but in 1919 I believed we were expanding too fast by far. During that year, the authorized capital stock was increased from $370,000,000 to $1,020,000,000. Less than a third of the common had been issued; nevertheless, on paper, the company had become a billion-dollar corporation. However, all my feeling, all my complaints, had to do with the physical expansion. Besides the tractor business, the company was taking over a variety of manufacturing enterprises. The corporation was getting many of its own sources of supply, of bodies, differential gears, and many other items. We were building new factories and putting up houses for employees. They were putting up a $20,000,000 office building. They kept buying things and budgeting this and budgeting that until it seemed, to me, we might come to a dismal ending. Buick was making about half the money, but the corporation was spending much faster than we could earn. So I quit—this time for keeps—saying, "Now, Billy, I'm done." Alfred Sloan and one other came to see me. Several years before, Alfred, after selling his Hyatt Roller Bearing Company to Durant, had become the president of a subsidiary company, which included Delco. They tried to talk me into staying.

"No, I'm washed up. I just can't stand the way the thing is being run. All I'm anxious about now is to sell my stock."

Again I was visited by Amory Haskell, as fine a gentleman as I ever met.

"Walt, we think we are going to buy the Citroën plant in France. We have bought sufficient exchange to make the deal and we are going soon. We want you to go along to look over the physical properties, so that you can give us a report from a mechanical standpoint."

"I've resigned, you know. If I can be of any use to General

161

Motors, I want to go. But it must be understood by you that I'm getting out."

"We'll talk about that later," said Mr. Haskell.

"What is this going to be, this boat ride?"

"Whatever you want it to be, Walt. Just come along."

When I told Della, she said, "We've waited a long time to have our first trip to Europe. If you are going, I want to go too."

"All right, honey; if I go, you go."

I reported this to Mr. Haskell. "How," he asked, "are we going to get passports?" I showed him the palms of my hands; it was his problem.

He arranged for them; not only for Mrs. Chrysler but for Mrs. Sloan, Mrs. Kettering and Mrs. Mott. Charles Stewart Mott was a vice-president of the corporation. Another who was in the party was Albert Champion, at that time head of the Champion Spark Plug Company. He was French by birth and spoke the language.

Many of the conversations we had on the boat were directed toward my staying in the corporation. If anyone could have persuaded me, it would have been Mr. Haskell; he was a wonderful man. I said: "I've tried two or three times to reconcile my views with those of Billy. Maybe he is right, maybe I'm right, but I am leaving. I have worked too hard and too many years in this automobile game to see what I have gained dissipated now."

That was a delightful trip, and the friendship of the Sloans and Chryslers, nourished in the intimacy of ships, hotels and on excursions, became a warm thing that continues to this day.

I saw the Citroën plant, every part of it, and my written report covered fifteen or twenty typewritten pages. But what that report might have said more crisply was, "You'd be crazy to buy it. You could equip a brand-new plant in France for what it would cost to modernize this old one according to American standards and in line with our scheme of quantity production. Moreover, there is not in France the necessary volume of business." The outcome was a decision not to buy Citroën. So the company, having bought French exchange to be ready to close a deal, proceeded to put the funds into American exchange. In the meantime dollars had gained over francs to such an extent that, I have been told, the company made $140,000 on our trip through exchange.

That year of 1919 I had been vice-president of General Motors in charge of operations, in addition to my role as president of Buick. I had been succeeded as general manager of Buick by Harry Bassett, an able fellow who had come with us in 1916, when the Weston-Mott Company was consolidated with Buick. He had become my assistant at that time, and he kept stepping right along behind me. When my resignation was official, he became the president of Buick and a vice-president of General Motors. When he died in 1926, the corporation lost a fine man.

Durant and Pierre du Pont did not want to see all my stock plumped on the market, so they started negotiations with me. I think the transaction was completed within two or three months after I had resigned.

I was going to retire—that is what I told my wife. I was forty-five. I had no plans of any kind, but I had given myself completely to my job for years, and, in consequence, I had neglected personal affairs. I had an investment problem, too, and that was why I wanted an office in Detroit. Yes, I was retired. I had nothing more to do, and wasn't that just fine and dandy!

The years had fixed on me a habit of becoming wide awake at six o'clock in the morning. So I'd get up and drive sixty-five miles to Detroit, fiddle around my office and then drive sixty-five miles back to Flint at night. Four or five days a week I would do that; the rest of the time I was hanging around the house. Men that I knew would come there to see me; old employees, friends of young days when I was making my living in overalls in roundhouses and shops, all sorts of people. When a new hotel was projected, the natural person to head the subscription list was the president of Buick, the town's outstanding industry. A new golf course? Get Walter Chrysler on the committee. Without a guard outside my door, necessarily that sort of thing increased when I was a man of leisure. Seemingly, the only men I knew were fellows who smoked. Our house, Mrs. Chrysler said, reeked of stale tobacco. She couldn't find a room where she could not hear the sound of deep male voices talking, talking, talking. Finally she spoke to me.

"I wish you would go to work." Because of her tone, I was relieved when she said "work." She added: "This isn't a home any more. It's just a place crowded with men. A sort of railroad station."

I grinned widely. She had said it first. It wouldn't seem like quitting on a promise if I changed my mind.

"Do you know what?" I said to her. "I will go back to work."

John N. Willys was in trouble in 1920; his Willys-Overland Company was in terrible shape. That year the company was making cars that not many people seemed to want. Yet, under the optimistic influence of the busy years of 1918 and 1919, when materials were hard to get and cars were easily sold, commitments had been made to take, during 1920, hundreds of thousands of bodies, tires and parts of all kinds, as well as new machine tools to shape these things into automobiles. Willys had plants at Toledo, Elmira and other places. On top of all this, he was building a big new plant over in Elizabeth, New Jersey. The company was headed for the rocks. Bankers wanted back the money they had loaned the company. These loans totaled more than $50,000,000.

The bankers, represented by a committee, came to me. One of its members was my old friend Ralph Van Vechten, of Chicago, who had loaned me the money to buy my first car. Willys wanted me, too, although matters had progressed to a point where he had no real say. I had known John since my early days at Buick; he had a paint plant in Flint and was often there. Repeatedly he had proposed that I come to work for him. His efforts in that direction had stopped, of course, when Billy Durant made me president of Buick and raised my pay to half a million. I was far from willing to plunge into the Willys-Overland problem. It was precisely because I had made a success at Buick, because of the reputation that I had earned there, that these fellows were asking me to try to save their money for them. Suppose I failed? What would such a failure do to my reputation? I did not have to go to work again. Why should I? When I raised this point, both Van Vechten and Willys took hold of me and argued. I told them then that I would make a proposition: I'd undertake the job for two years at a million dollars a year, net.

The bankers, figuring that their money was gone unless a miracle happened, directed John to accept my terms. It was further agreed, because of my insistence, that I was to have full charge. John was to keep his title, but he was to treat me as the doctor. My title was executive vice-president. When that was settled in black and white, I went to work. Expenses had to be cut; that was clear to all. That was when I moved to New York. I was at the Biltmore first; then we had an apartment in the Carlton House.

One day right after I took hold, I walked into John's office. You never saw another like it; magnificent. John had been a great go-getter from his beginning in the bicycle business. In his office there was a splendid humidor, ornate with gold, a huge affair, richly stocked with fine cigars. John led me to the table which supported this luxurious chest. He raised the lid and pressed me to have a cigar. I took one that must have cost fifty cents and lighted it. Then, when our cigars were burning, I spoke.

"John, I am here to cut your salary." He was drawing $150,000 a year.

"What's this, Walt?" John looked at me as an actor does when another muffs his lines.

"I'm cutting you to $75,000 a year."

He gave his head a little toss, and then he laughed. "I guess we've put our problems in the right man's hands," he said.

I had a tough job, and John knew it; his whole establishment had been running wild while John had been away. Bad management sometimes means a lot of things I would not wish to discuss. Anyway, the lesson of those boom days has been well learned by all the automobile companies that I know anything about.

All that was bad in the Willys-Overland Corporation was due, really, to lack of competition, to the wartime boom and its easy money. Prosperity had made some of its officials too tolerant of things that, in any better managed corporation, would have been regarded as shocking. Willys himself had been away too much and certain of his subordinates had got out of hand. We knew what expenditures were proper, what were not, and required some executives to restore money which they had, in my opinion, squandered. But the greatest service we were able to perform was in adjusting all those too optimistic commitments for parts—for everything from tires to bodies. Of course, because of my years at Buick, the task of compromising all those commitments was much simpler for me than it would have been for any banker. The manufacturers felt, with good reason, that for one order they agreed to cancel, they might look for vastly bigger orders in the uncharted but promising future. They knew, too, that it would be poor business strategy to enforce any contract that would help destroy a customer who was in trouble. Besides, in dealing with me, it was useless for any of them to say that cancellation meant hardship unless it were really true. I traveled everywhere that parts were made, talked over long-distance telephone wires until my voice became hoarse; argued; cajoled; and in a few months I had cut the company's debt by millions.

A lot of things had been going on inside that vast and sprawling corporation that had wholly escaped the attention of its management.

One day, when I was thinking about that enterprise, my secretary broke in and said, "There's an Army officer out here." She gave his name.

I remembered him well. I had met him in Washington during the war. He had been a tough, hard, fierce-eyed baby with red hair. Once, for three days, I had wrestled with him over a shell contract. I was an industrialist; he was an Army officer. I wanted that contract to do certain things for the corporation I represented. I thought we were entitled to them; he did not. Could I fool him? Not by any shape that I could give my arguments. Finally, when I was leaving his office, I had spoken to him pretty freely:

"Listen; if I can't have this contract the way I want it you can—well, give it to some manufacturer who isn't so well acquainted with his costs. But I got to tell you that you are smart—mind, I'm smiling—but you are smart. And tough."

"A compliment, Mr. Chrysler." ·

"You bet it's a compliment. And say, when this war is over, if you ever want a job, come and say so. I'll hire you."

Well, the war was over and there was this colonel, standing in my office in civilian clothes. As he came in the door he had called out, "Remember me?"

"Remember you? How can I ever forget you?" I cussed him affectionately and saw him grin.

"You said if I ever needed a job ——"

"What salary do you want, colonel?"

"I've just spent about a year losing what money I had, trying to get somewhere in the rubber business. You fix the salary."

"You're hired."

Just that quickly I had a general purchasing agent for the future. I knew three things about him: He was honest; he was loyal; he had ability. That is all I ask from any man. I don't care how raw the ability is; that can be developed through experience. But unless a man is loyal and honest, I don't want him associated with me.

The first job I handed to him was as tough as anything he ever saw in the Army. I sent for him about three days after he went on the pay roll, gave him the name of this company, told him what kind of things it made and what city it was in. Then I said, "It's rotten. That's all I can tell you. I want you to go there, stay a month or six weeks, and then come back and tell me what's wrong."

"Fine," said the colonel. "I know less about that kind of business than any other you could specify. So, I'll have plenty of curiosity."

"You know as much about it as I do. Tomorrow you'll know a lot more. What I say is, it's rotten. When you can, report back why it is that way."

In a little while the colonel was bossing that plant. We fired the president, and under the colonel it began to run so smoothly that I never bothered with his report. But he found out plenty; I know that. Eventually, the colonel was to become general purchasing agent for the Chrysler Corporation, after it had been expanded to include Dodge. He has spent millions and millions of dollars for us, and you couldn't any more fool him in 1936 than back in 1917. After 1929 that former Army officer has been running our truck business and some other divisions of the Chrysler Corporation. He can handle any kind of a job.

I might have cited any one of a score of my associates in order to highlight the significance of what was shaping in my mind when I hired this man, Col. A. C. Downey. I wanted men that I could work with, full of confidence in their integrity. From the day that I had left Flint to go to New York, I had been aware that for my purposes men were what I wanted. One whose name was engraved on my mind as I left Flint was K. T. Keller. That young man was a production man after my own heart. However, I did not let myself think too much of Keller then, nor of others that I was leaving. One thing I never have done: I never have broken down one organization to build up another. I have been sensible of a strong obligation to anything that has ever held my loyalty. Consequently, I had gone from Flint knowing that I was leaving many men whose talents, character and companionship I would be hungering for in my future work, whatever it might be. Yet I think I never hired a man away from Buick. As months went on, many of them came to see me and asked for jobs. However much I yearned to have them, I would say, "Better stay where you are. You've got a good job. There's no telling what's in store for me." To those whose qualities I admired, I always added: "But any time you are out of a job, come and see me. Then we'll have a talk."

However, in those first months away from Flint I met some other men.

The Willys-Overland Corporation had saddled itself with an airplane plant, with a harvester company and with other subsidiaries, almost none of which were doing it any good. But its harvesters and airplanes, if anything, were rather better than its automobiles. The company had to make better automobiles if it was to survive. Over in Elizabeth it had an unfinished plant, quite new. Some of the bankers' millions had gone into that place, which was vast. What could be made by Willys that would sell? At that time I had agreed with John Willys that we would add a new car to the line. That was how it happened that I met Zeder and Skelton and Breer.

Those three young automotive engineers were wizards. They seemed to be the parts of a single, extraordinary engineering intelligence; their names were Fred M. Zeder, Owen Skelton and Carl Breer. You never would find, hunt high or low, three friends more harmoniously attuned, unless it might be those men of fiction, the Three Musketeers.

Zeder, a graduate of the University of Michigan, had been on his way to becoming chief engineer of the Studebaker Corporation when, in 1909, he encountered Breer, just out of Leland Stanford, Jr., University and beginning an apprenticeship at Allis-Chalmers. Skelton, a graduate of the engineering school of Ohio State University, was then with Packard, in the designing rooms, where he was known as a talented expert on transmissions and axles. His first job had been with Pope-Toledo as early as 1905. Zeder brought these two men into the Studebaker engineering department, and there they worked until 1920. I knew them to be star engineers, brilliant in the field of automobile designing.

I had a corner of the Elizabeth plant partitioned off for them. They were the ones who were going to design the new car, the one that would take the place of the mechanical "boggle" that, I had felt, would complete the ruin of the Willys Company if it were produced. I soon found myself running over to New Jersey pretty frequently. Those engineers spoke to each other almost without using words, so well did they understand one another. But what was thrilling was to discover that they understood me too. Whereas John Willys sometimes seemed to feel that the company's problems could be met by a couple of new gadgets and a coat of paint, I was convinced that the country was waiting for a better automobile than had yet been offered to it.

What was my future going to be? I had determined that I was going to make somewhere, somehow, a kind of automobile that—I was beginning to feel pretty strongly—was unlikely to be made in the Willys plants. I commissioned Zeder, Skelton and Breer to proceed with the designing of the automobile about which they had been dreaming. They had set themselves up as a firm of consultant engineers in an old building in Mechanic Street in Newark. There they had moved their staff, their drafting tools and other implements of their profession. I used to see them there, and what we had to talk about was wholly exciting. Necessarily and properly, the unfinished blueprints of what they had been designing at Elizabeth they had left behind them. We believed that was a better car than was running on the highways, but it had to be left out of calculation, for a while at least. That was to become Billy Durant's Flint car. In the meantime, my banker friends had asked me to help them in another troublesome situation. This time it was the Maxwell Motors Company that was in distress.

·VIII·

REWARDS FOR A WORKMAN

1924

"They Knew This Car Was a Sensation"

· VIII ·
REWARDS FOR A WORKMAN

RIGHT after the war all automobile companies had experienced a boom market. Customers asked salesmen
only one tough question, "Can you make delivery?" If you
could deliver automobiles you could sell them. For a little
while this demand had helped some companies to overcome
the effects of abrupt cancellation of Government contracts.
Impressed by these conditions, bankers had continued to extend credit to the Maxwell Motor Company until the total of
its debt was $26,000,000. Then what had appeared to be a
flourishing boom ended in a depression, the postwar collapse.

James Cox Brady was one who approached me on behalf of
the bankers. Jim and his brother Nicholas had become my
warm friends. I was eager to oblige them, and they made
their urgings stronger by getting the consent of Willys for me
to undertake the reorganization of Maxwell while still working to straighten out Willys-Overland. So I became the chairman of the Maxwell reorganization and management committee.

Although the Bradys hoped to see me continue with Maxwell, I was far from sure about it. The Maxwell had been
in a disagreeable fight with Chalmers, on which it had a
lease, and there was such an entanglement of intercompany

disputes that I began to believe it would be a mistake to associate myself for long with Maxwell. Once I remember leaving a meeting and saying, "I would not touch it with a ten-foot pole." What I was saying I would not touch was later on revealed to be the greatest opportunity of my whole life. However, the Bradys held me to my word, and in the meantime one of my frinds gave me some good advice.

"Now, Walter," he began, "it seems to me that Maxwell is what you have been searching for; here it is right in your hand. But you must change your ideas of compensation. You got half a million salary from General Motors and you got a million a year from Willys—because the bankers were desperate. This is different. You are more than a production man now; you have revealed yourself to be a merchandiser, and you are revealing capacity in finance too. If you will collect your reward in the future, through ownership and its attendant satisfactions, you will fare better than ever before. But the salary ought not to be more than $100,000."

I agreed, and I was given, besides, a contract of employment and options on a large block of stock.

There was about a year when I was spending a good many nights on trains between New York and Detroit. Often those trips were made with Nick and Jim Brady, my good friends; we had grand times together. But I never shall forget the way the banking committee heard how I proposed to get their money back for them, out of this company of which they had become the not-too-happy owners.

"What! Lend Maxwell another $15,000,000? Have a heart, Walter!"

"Now wait a minute until you hear what I have to say. I want to pay off the creditors by giving them five millions in cash now, and for the balance of the debt, one, two and three year notes at six per cent. That gives the company a three-year breathing spell. If you want to save Maxwell——"

"What about the rest of these fifteen millions?"

"Wait a little until you hear what I have to say. You want to get your money back, don't you?"

"Sure! We want back the twenty-six millions already loaned."

"That money is in the plants in the form of materials, much of it in finished parts. When this is manufactured into automobiles that can be sold, you'll start getting your money back."

"But what about these other millions you want us to lend?"

"I'll need that money to operate the company. But the car, as it is, won't sell. I'm arranging for its redesign. I'm going to cut the price."

"How much?" They all had their pencils out.

I had put a price of $995 on the redesigned car; that showed a profit of only $5.

"Walter, you're crazy. You can't sell automobiles for a five-dollar profit."

"I'm liquidating an inventory."

"But $5 on a car! It ought to be $100."

"Listen, we can move them at $995. Charge $100 more and they won't move. Not these cars!"

After Maxwell and Chalmers had been put through a friendly receivership we bought all the assets, Harry Bronner and I, for the account of the reorganization and management committee. The Maxwell cars, redesigned, at $995 were selling at a satisfactory rate, and actually the company's situation, braced by the fresh millions of capital, was greatly improved. However, on paper it was something we often had to defend.

My friend, B. E. Hutchinson, did most of the defending after he came to Maxwell in the summer of 1922, as its treasurer. Hutch had begun his work with us by writing out of our list of assets items that totaled about $11,000,000. Minus that amount the picture we presented when we asked for credit was somewhat less rosy, yet it inspired a respect that began to grow. For that our corporation owes a lot to Hutch. He was just a young fellow then, about thirty-four; he was a Chicago boy who had gone, at sixteen, from Hyde Park High School to Massachusetts Institute of Technology. After two years, a part of which he worked as a reporter on the staff of the Boston Globe, he was back in Illinois, working with a shovel around the steel furnaces of the Grand Crossing Tack Company. When he was twenty-two he had become superintendent of the open-hearth department there. He had varied experiences in industry until, in 1918, he joined the staff of Ernst & Ernst, certified public accountants. It is Hutch I have in mind when, occasionally, I find myself advising the son of some old friend. Lately such a boy wanted me to help him get a job with an airplane company.

"You come to me for advice?"

"Yes, sir."

"All right, son, you are going to get some: Aviation, as you say, is a developing industry, but from what I can hear there are scores of youngsters after every job it has to offer. Why don't you get yourself into a field that gives you a chance to discover all kinds of chances, in or out of aviation? You know this country is filled with developing industries. And there are lots of chances. You simply want to make yourself smart enough to recognize them before the other fellow does. If I were you, I'd qualify myself for accountancy. I'd become an accountant. Young accountants are sent around by their firms to audit the books of companies everywhere. They have a skill that makes them mighty valuable in business; indispensable. They often get chances to go to work for the companies whose books they have audited."

B. E. Hutchinson is a perfect illustration of my argument. Because he was well qualified Ernst & Ernst, in 1918, sent him to take charge of the reorganization of accounting and system of the American Writing Paper Company; a little later, when the assignment was finished, he became treasurer of the company. But his big chance came when the Maxwell Motor Corporation was being reorganized. No more big opportunities in this country? There never were so many opportunities for young men in the history of the world. If you miss one chance, that is no reason for brooding; there will be another if you keep alert and qualify yourself for opportunities.

I believed I had missed a great opportunity late in the spring of 1922. My work with Willys was finished. The bankers had arranged for a $16,500,000 bond issue to retire the Willys-Overland loan, and the company was being put through a receivership. As a part of the cleaning-up process the big, idle plant over in Elizabeth was to be sold at auction. The banks knew it represented about $14,000,000 of their money, but were ready to take whatever they could get for it. Our car was to be sold with the plant; that is, the blueprints of that car that Zeder, Skelton and Breer and their associates had designed.

"You could buy that new Elizabeth plant for Maxwell for much less than it cost, Walter." One of the committee was tempting me. He knew the inside of the Willys situation and the inside of the Maxwell situation. He knew it was difficult to exercise leadership where there was so much bickering between groups of stockholders, bondholders and other kinds of creditors. I don't think he realized how much I had been disappointed at the failure of the Willys Corporation to bring out the car.

I did not go to the auction myself, but had a representative on hand. He had authority to bid somewhat more than $5,000,000. But among the bidders was Billy Durant! Billy had been in the Elizabeth plant several times during that spring, had been there without any blaring of trumpets. He had been shown three cars in which this new motor was mounted. There, in the vast spaces of that plant, he had ridden in one. Billy topped bid after bid and kept on until the representatives of General Motors and Maxwell had ceased to bid. Durant paid $5,525,000 for the plant and got a bargain.

Durant arranged with Zeder, Skelton, Breer and their associates to design and furnish the drawings for a motor of the same type but of a little larger size. Billy was convinced it had to be larger, to have greater horsepower. He brought it out as the Flint, and it was an excellent car. The trouble was that the price necessarily was high. In the Elizabeth plant he began building another car, one to compete with Ford. It was called the Star, and before other difficulties overwhelmed Billy Durant there were 1,500,000 Star cars on the highways of the country.

What a blessing in disguise my disappointment was! With the first car transformed into Billy Durant's Flint, we had more time to appreciate the possibilities of that other car on which Zeder had been working with Skelton, Breer and me. Although we experienced a good deal of frustration, building piecemeal as we were required to do, nevertheless a couple of these cars were made, a part here, a part there, until they were complete—and costly. We tested them on the roads too. Those were exciting times.

Under an old car's shabby hood we had hidden the unsuspected power of our new high-compression engine. Zeder and his boys had outdone themselves. You could tell that any time a traffic cop's uplifted palm stopped you in a group of cars. It was the most fun if this shabby old testing car was halted between a couple of big ones, with snooty chauffeurs at their wheels. At the whistle's sound we would be past the cop and on our way, while behind us, open-mouthed, our chance rivals would just be getting ready to go into second gear. What flexibility we had! That is, by contrast with any other car that rolled upon the highways back in 1923. The Chrysler car? Nobody had heard about a Chrysler car. But we had dreamed about it until, as if we had been its lovers, it was work to think of anything else.

Any time I vanished from New York to go to that drab little factory building in Mechanic Street on a Friday, as had become my habit, I would be lost to my family for the several days of the week end. I'd call my wife, apologize and start to explain, when she would interrupt to mock me: "Yes, I know. You're in New Jersey and you're going to stay through Sunday." Then, quickly, her voice would change. "Of course I understand. Go ahead and stay."

Eventually, however, Zeder, Skelton and Breer were established in the old Chalmers plant at Detroit; we had it all cleaned out and renovated. We were no longer fretting about broken-down companies; we were thinking about plants and how they could be used. The new Maxwell board had taken over that mechanical infant that we had been nursing, Zeder's high-compression engine. This was to be the heart of our new car. After their several brave years of working in the face of much frustration it was a joy to turn over to the engineers the money the board had authorized as payment and to bring them, as a unit, into the organization to direct its engineering. Naturally, by then, I was in the enterprise with all my heart and soul. It was already determined that the new car on which our hopes were founded would be called the Chrysler. That was about the time I got a jolt from my friend Nick Brady.

"Walter," he said, "Jim is desperately ill. I hate to be tied up in the automobile business at a time like this. We hope to make a deal with Studebaker."

I felt sick; but the Bradys were my friends, and so without any debate I agreed to toss in my options and cancel my contract of employment, provided an arrangement was worked out that would be acceptable to the other stockholders. It was clear that if Studebaker bought out the Bradys, then Frederick S. Fish, chairman of Studebaker, would want to head up the combined enterprises with the Studebaker president, Albert R. Erskine. There would hardly be room for Erskine and Chrysler in one pasture lot.

Happily for me, that deal fell through, and once more I was burning with enthusiasm for what was going on in the old Chalmers plant.

Then came bad news that was not a false alarm. Two banking firms had agreed, several months before the New York Automobile Show of January, 1924, to take $6,000,000 of the Maxwell Company's bonds at 92; that would net us $5,520,000. Hutch and I had believed this was a settled matter until the bankers, with regrets and apologies galore, explained that they believed it wise to cancel the arrangement. That was a tough situation!

On top of that we got the disheartening information that while the American Automobile Chamber of Commerce would, of course, allot space in which to show the 1924 models of the Maxwell cars, the rules forbade allotment of space to models of a car which had not been produced and sold. Our Chrysler models were barred from the show! We had counted heavily upon creating a sensation with our new car. Through the public's reaction to its smarter lines, to its smooth and vastly greater power, we had hoped to make the bankers change their minds about the loan. Already we had stretched our credit to the snapping point, for it is never a cheap operation to retool a factory for a mass-production operation; nor can the work be done without months of preparation. We could not sell Chrysler cars unless we made them. We could not hope to proceed with the making unless our feeble credit was made strong with money from the bankers. It seemed to us that we were pretty close to ruin before we had made a start. Of course, none of my associates know the meaning of the word quit, but this was a major crisis in our campaign.

The whole executive staff of the organization was there. Hutch was looking at me, solemnly. Without discussion we knew what this might do to our credit position despite the tireless work of Hutch to make it strong; we could expect it to hit our credit like a dynamite explosion. The bad news spread swiftly through our suite of rooms and I dreaded seeing Fred Zeder and his two partners, Breer and Skelton. I knew how they would feel, because I felt the same way. A large part of the thrill after creating a great new automobile comes through professional pride when you show it, with all your understanding friends and rivals crowding around, yarning about your "job." The great talents of this trio of engineers had given our beautiful car terrific power, style and grace. If we failed to show it they would be bitterly disappointed, and so would I, in ways more subtle than any commercial loss.

Suddenly I began to yell for Joe. That was J. E. Fields, who today is vice-president of the Chrysler Corporation and an important factor in the executive management. He was our sales manager then, a good-looking fellow and a great salesman. He had started selling machinery in Fargo, North

Dakota, and gone from there to the National Cash Register Company. When Hugh Chalmers left his big job there to organize the Chalmers Company in 1909, Joe Fields was one of those who helped him do it. Then Joe had gone with Hupmobile, directing its selling, but when I took charge of Maxwell-Chalmers he came back. We needed him because he knew every dealer in the country. Well, this time I wanted Joe because he was a fellow who never has learned how to take "no" for an answer.

Grand Central Palace, where the New York Automobile Show is held, is where the public pays admissions to see the year's new cars, but the men of the automobile industry always swarm in some near-by hotel; that year their rendezvous was the Hotel Commodore.

"Joe, you've hired plenty of hotel rooms. Go and hire the lobby of the Commodore. We'll have a show all right!"

Joe Fields did not stop to ask any questions; he simply vanished. When he came back he fluttered a sheet of hotel stationery with some writing on it. "Boss," he said, "we own the lobby."

Although we were not in the show, we stole it! From morning until late at night a crowd was densely packed around us. Even before the end of that first eventful day we knew that our models were attracting more attention than was being excited by anything on display in Grand Central Palace. All our old friends of the trade came to speak to us in the lobby, to shake our hands and poke us in the ribs.

"Seventy miles an hour? Is that on the level, Walt?" There were shrewd brains behind some of the eyes that were looking our new six over, inside and out. Now and then I would observe a rival manufacturer pass his fingers over the plush-covered seats, and I would know that he was adding to his mental computation upholstery at $6 a yard. They knew this car was a sensation, but what they most wished to know was its retail price. A high-compression engine was something all automobile men appreciated, but, until our car had appeared, they had treated it as a racing driver's luxury that would be offered to the public far in the future. Yet here it was all ready to compete with what they had to offer. That was why they were so wild with curiosity about the Chrysler six's price. But we were keeping that a secret.

Then there came what we were waiting for, a nice, plump banker, an acquaintance.

"Your new car is attracting lots of favorable comment, Walter."

"You like it?"

"Oh, indeed, yes. Wheel base is rather short."

"We don't think so; it's an advantage in parking, you know, and it is 160 inches over all. Moreover, this car has improved springing."

I was trying manfully to keep from showing any eagerness. Yet this banker had the means to give us what we so desperately needed.

As I talked with him the car exhibits were only a part of the show we were putting on there in the lobby of the Commodore. The rest of it was what we were doing by pretending to be carefree. Watching me you would have thought I did not know how to worry. But the banker was clearing his throat.

"We are willing to take five millions of Maxwell bonds."

"What price?"

"Seventy."

My heart seemed to drop down on my stomach. Then I got mad. Seventy! Why, that meant that by mortgaging itself for $5,000,000 Maxwell would get only $3,500,000. In a few minutes he was walking away, having no doubts whatever as to how I felt about his offer. There were other bankers in the lobby, and some of them spoke to me.

Ed Tinker, who was then president of the Chase Securities Corporation, was the next one who talked business. We dickered, seated inside the car, with the doors closed and a ring of faces staring at us as if we had been fish in a bowl.

I wanted ninety-six, I told Tinker.

"You'd have taken ninety-two, and glad to get it, Walt, a few months ago."

"Ed, these people are wild about this car. It's got qualities they can't buy in a $5000 automobile."

"You'll sell this car all right, Walt. Ninety-four, I guess if we get a bonus ——"

"Ninety-six, Ed. And no bonus."

"Mister, if you don't let me out of this automobile right this instant I'll scream." Ed was mocking me with a voice that he had transformed into a shrill falsetto of a desperate woman.

"Ninety-six."

"Ninety-four; and I'm going downtown right now."

Ed Tinker went, and suddenly I was scared. Suppose he changed his mind? Suppose some of his associates at Chase Securities disagreed? Suppose the offer of ninety-four should be withdrawn? The situation had become overpowering. I knew we had to settle matters then and there. I looked around for our young treasurer.

"Hutch, we're going down and clinch this offer."

Down in the Wall Street district Hutch and I stood on the curbstone across the street from the bank.

"I'll stay here while you go in, Hutch."

He crossed the street and vanished. I stayed on the curb.

186

It was a blustery January day, but it was not the cold that made me shiver as I waited. I waited long too.

Tinker, I learned later, was not at his desk when Hutch arrived. He had gone out. Where? Second floor, to the barbershop.

Hutch took up the trail and found Ed reclining in the chair of a private little one-man shop, his face hidden under a mask of lather.

"We'll take your ninety-four," said Hutch, and straight up rose Mr. Tinker. "That is," said Hutch, "we can take it if you'll close with us today. Important matters require us to have your yes or no immediately. Mr. Chrysler sends you word that it's now—or never."

Tinker wiped the lather off, put on his coat and with Hutchinson returned to his office.

"Three o'clock is the deadline," said Hutch.

"That's all right," Tinker assured him. "I think we'll make the deal."

"But Mr. Chrysler has to know by three o'clock."

When Hutch came back to me his eyes were shining, and when I had his news we went into a near-by cigar store to a public telephone. I asked for Albert Rathbone, of Larkin, Rathbone and Perry, our lawyers, but soon found myself talking with Rathbone's partner, Nicholas Kelly.

"Kelly, you got to get that mortgage signed by five o'clock tonight."

"It is almost three o'clock now, Mr. Chrysler."

"I don't care. Can't take any chances. Everything depends on this."

"All right. We'll get right after it, but it takes time to draw up a contract."

"Get started."

Hutchinson and Kelly, with men from the office of Rushmore, Bisbee & Stern, lawyers for the Chase bank, worked all through the evening. At midnight they got a fresh recruit. Eldon Bisbee arrived from some public dinner; he was in his dress clothes, white tie, white waistcoat. At six o'clock in the morning they were still at work and all of us saw the sun come up.

A very little while later the contract was executed and what was already, in my heart, the Chrysler Corporation, but still called Maxwell, was out of the woods. We had our money, we had our car and we had a live organization.

All through the week Joe Fields had been nagging me to tell him the price of the new car. He was enthusiastic, but he was realistic too.

"That short wheel base, you know, is going to make them expect a bargain." The wheel base was 113¾ inches.

"They will be getting a bargain, Joe. It's plenty long enough, and it will be much easier to park than these longer cars. That's what you want to tell your dealers."

"Say, I can get orders for this car right now. My arm would be tired just from writing, if only I knew the price —and if the price was right."

I wrote something on a card then and handed it to Joe. As I walked away I saw that his big black eyebrows were rising toward his gray hair. The price I had fixed was the same as Buick, $1595.

Events proved that it was not too much. In the next few months Joe's forces began to sell them about as fast as we were able to roll the cars off the line, in what had been the old Chalmers plant. But I was determined that we were going to give better and better values in the years to come.

There was no question about space for the Chrysler sixes when the allotments were made for the Automobile Show of 1925. In one year we had sold 32,000 of them, in addition to which there had been a sharp gain in the sales of the Maxwell fours. The result for that year, which we began by creating a debt of $5,000,000, was a net profit of $4,115,000. It was a good time to straighten out our corporation structure and so, in 1925, the Maxwell Motor Corporation became the Chrysler Corporation. That was about the time, it seems to me, that I had an interesting conversation with some of my banker friends.

Some of them had stock which they had taken in the reorganization, in place of wiped-out debts. But when the stock got to sixteen the bankers could get out with a whole skin, and out they got, against my urging.

"Listen," I protested, "you have seen this thing come up from nothing. Aren't you foolish to sell now, just when you might hope for profit?"

"That's not the way we do business. We loaned money and the loan went sour. We were in the hole and now we're out."

They meant it too. Whatever stock they sold I bought. I bought an awful lot of stock at fifteen and sixteen, stock that later was split so that I got four for one.

That was about the time we got K. T. Keller in the Chrysler Corporation. He had wanted to come along when I left Buick and General Motors, but I had said, "Stay here and whenever I see a job that will pay you enough, I'll send for you." After that, K. T. had become vice-president of Chevrolet, in charge of manufacturing; then he had become general manager of the Canadian Division of General Motors.

He was up in Canada when I sent him word in the winter of 1926 that I would like to see him at the Chicago Automobile Show.

When Keller came I was standing beside our show exhibit, and if you had seen us you might have supposed it was just a casual conversation; but it was a warm reunion, for we two are kindred spirits.

"I've never had a job to offer you before," I said, "but now I can make you a real offer." I told him what I could pay and then I asked, "Do you want to come with me?"

"Sure," he said. I made him general manager of Chrysler. He was precisely what we needed then, a great production man.

There were four Chrysler models in 1926; a "50," a "60," a "70" (the original Chrysler in its improved form), and an Imperial "80." The next year saw us in fifth place in the industry, with sales of 192,000 automobiles. That was 1927, ten years ago. You might have supposed there was not a cloud on the horizon. Well, I was pretty happy, I'll admit. A splendid corporation had spread itself around the world. Nevertheless, we could see that competition month by month was getting tougher.

The primer lesson of the automobile business was: "Make your product so that all American families can afford to buy it." Now and again some manufacturer would seem to forget that lesson. But we were not forgetting it. Each time we expanded our activities so as to make some part we had previously been buying from an outside manufacturer, we had been able to lower prices. The automobile business has grown to what it is by steadily and rigorously eliminating waste from all its manufacturing processes. We had bought another plant across the street from Chalmers; in this one, the Kercheval, we were making bodies. But we were still forced to buy too many parts outside. We were reminded of that each time we tried to get our Chrysler "50" on a better basis to compete with Dodge.

We were then compelled to buy all of our cast-iron parts because we had no foundries. Dodge had a big foundry. We were paying out vast sums for forged parts, too, because we had no forge shop. Dodge had a big forge shop; Dodge had many plants filled with things for lack of which our products were costing more than was necessary. Moreover, without the better control of costs such as we could achieve with bigger plants, there was no hope of dipping into that greatest of automobile markets, the one in which Henry Ford's only real rival was the Chevrolet.

We had done plenty of figuring, and knew that to exercise our full manufacturing power and talents we would have to acquire plants that would cost, if we had to build them, about $75,000,000. Where and how were we going to round up that kind of money? Every time we gave the matter thought, we found our heads full of visions of the splendid plants of the Dodge brothers. The Dodge brothers had passed away, but they had left a splendid name in the industry. They had been manufacturers for whom I had great respect. In the beginning they were making automobile parts for Henry Ford, and when they began making Dodge cars, in the same year that war broke out in Europe, they still had their minds focused on Ford, which was sensible of them. What they made was a rugged mechanism that could be counted on to get over the roughest kinds of road, and to keep on going even after you came to the end of the road. While the Dodge brothers lived, a Dodge car almost invariably cost just about $100 more than a Ford, and those who admired it above any other car they could afford represented a generous share of the automobile market. But in the year that I was hired by bankers to take charge of Willys-Overland, both John and Horace Dodge died, about ten or eleven months apart. Four years later their widows agreed to sell the business to the New York banking house of Dillon, Read & Company, and Clarence Dillon signed a check for $146,-000,000.

I had become acquainted with Clarence some time after that event.

One day he walked into my office and asked me if I felt like doing some trading.

"Hell, Clarence, I don't want your plant. What'll I do with it?"

Clarence is a good salesman. He did not leave right away. Of course we wanted that plant, and I don't think I fooled him much. I let him talk for a couple of hours. We knew about the plants; I think we knew rather more about them than Clarence. But I listened pretty sharply when he tried to excite my envy discussing the handpicked sales organization that had been inherited from the Dodge brothers. They had always boasted that it was the best sales force in the industry. However, I never let Clarence discover my eagerness, and finally he stood up to go.

"Walter, I'm going back downtown and talk this over with my associates."

"All right, Clarence. Come in again, anytime."

In three or four days he was back and wanted to tell me more. I was gruff and short on this occasion.

"It's too much money. We aren't interested. Of course, if it was a bargain—but it's not. So what's the use of talking?"

"Now, Walt, don't shut your eyes to this. How else are you going to make the Chrysler Corporation into a first-rank competitor of Henry Ford or General Motors?"

"Clarence, we're doing pretty well. Can you show me another company with a record to compare with the Chrysler Corporation? We've been getting better, year by year."

"That's true, Walter, but I've been watching and you've

192

got your head pretty close to the ceiling right now, unless——"

"It's too much money, Clarence. You keep right on worrying about Dodge. Maybe it will come on the market a whole lot cheaper next year, or the year after. When a big outfit like that starts slipping it can go down fast."

"Dodge isn't slipping, Walter."

"I hear different."

"They got a fine name. They have had a fine product year after year."

"Sure, Clarence. I know. You paid $30,000,000 just for the goodwill. But that was when the company was making lots of money. How're you doing now?"

"We're doing splendidly. Only I think your crowd could do much better with it."

Clarence kept supplying me with scraps of information during a month or six weeks. Then, one day, he strode into my office and began to moan.

"Walter, bankers got no business trying to run a great big industrial enterprise. What do I know about making automobiles and selling them? That's your game. Why don't you take this Dodge business?"

I looked at him for about a minute before I spoke.

"Clarence, I haven't time to talk endlessly. You are wasting your time and you are wasting mine. Do you really want to trade? Then put your proposition down on a piece of paper. Mind, your lowest price! And don't forget: I'm not making the proposition; you are bringing it to me. So you had better make it tempting. Set your price and then I'll tell you, yes or no."

Clarence said he would arrive at a price and then come back.

Already, I could see, he was doing sums in his head. Before he was out on the street I was talking to Hutchinson in

Detroit. Hutch was directing a great big job of figuring that was going on behind the scenes. This was going to be more than an ordinary trade. H. A. Davies was working with him; he had been assistant treasurer when I took over the management of Maxwell and had been shoulder to shoulder with Hutch when we were establishing credit relations with banks all over the country. Hutch and Davies were adding up everything we knew about Dodge, so that we would be prepared when the dickering started. I did not see Clarence again for ten days or so, but when he did come he brought some typewritten sheets on which he had everything figured out. That was when I brought in Hutch and called up Albert Rathbone, our lawyer. Dillon was drawing up a chair, right beside my desk.

"Not here, Clarence."

"What?"

"Not here. I'm bringing two people into this conference and you can bring a couple for yourself. You may get a sore throat from talking before we've finished."

"Where do you want to talk?"

"We'll go over to the Ritz and get a suite of rooms, and, Clarence, we'll stay in that suite until we come to a conclusion, stay until one of us says yes or no."

From the start of our negotiations we insisted that Dillon would have to get the holders of ninety per cent of the Dodge stock to agree to the plan; we were quite certain that we did not want to merge ourselves with a disgruntled minority.

"Ninety per cent of all classes of stock, Clarence, or else ——"

"All right, Walter. Give me time enough."

"Two months. If we give you longer, the time for creating new car models will be on us and passed before the new management can get a chance to function."

We stayed there in that Ritz suite, arguing, eating, smoking, sleeping, talking, trading, until five days had gone. When we finished, all of us had bloodshot eyes from weariness; but we also knew a feeling of triumph. The terms provided that the Chrysler Corporation should pay $170,-000,000 in new Chrysler stock and in the assumption of Dodge debentures. However, all of this necessarily hung in the balance for the two months during which Clarence was to obtain the acquiesence of the holders of ninety per cent of the Dodge stock. Our session in the Ritz, as I recall it, was the end of May, and several times, the latter part of July, Clarence came around to ask for an extension of that time limit which we regarded as crucial for the effective fulfillment of our merger plans. Then when we were about forty-eight hours from the deadline Clarence begged for an extension. He was lacking 60,000 shares, he said, of meeting that ninety per cent requirement.

"Clarence, I can't do a thing for you. I can't do something for you at the expense of the Chrysler stockholders. You know that."

"Great grief, Walter, I've got eighty-five per cent of the stock. That's more than is ever brought in on a deal of this kind."

"We'll agree on that, Mr. Dillon," said Albert Rathbone, "but this is another deal. We said ninety per cent. You agreed."

"But, Walter, you want to make this deal."

"Yes, on the terms agreed upon."

"Here's what I'm up against: One of the large stockholders is in Paris. She cannot get that stock into our hands in two days. That's why I can't put my hands on those 60,000 shares of preferred." Bankers unemotional? You should have heard and seen Clarence!

"Clarence, when the day comes we ring the bell, and the deal is off unless you deliver."

"Walter, I can't do it in two days."

"Clarence," I said, using emphatic words, "it has not been a matter of two days. It has been sixty days, lacking two. I think you can do it. But if you can't, the deal is off."

As Clarence rushed out of the office, seemingly in despair, even my own lawyers seemed to be looking at me with reproachful eyes. Yet there was a happy ending, because Clarence, before the time limit expired, somehow produced the 60,000 shares. That deal was closed July 31, 1928.

Next morning Clarence came around to smoke a cigarette with me and give me assurance we could let that great Dodge organization run itself, oh, for three months if we wanted to.

"Hell, Clarence," I said, "our boys moved in last night." They had, too, with K. T. Keller in command. Just before five o'clock in the afternoon, as the papers were signed, I had picked up the phone to talk with Keller in Detroit.

"We've bought the Dodge," I told him. "Put up your signs."

Those canvas signs, prepared several days before, bore this legend: CHRYSLER CORPORATION, DODGE DIVISION. Squads of Keller's men had the signs in big trucks, and when he got my word Keller gave them the signal to nail them up on the Dodge plants. At the same time Keller, with half a dozen of his men, entered the Dodge headquarters and told the president of Dodge that we were running the plant from that moment. The next minute we were running it and the Chrysler Corporation, by that act, had become a larger organization by five or six fold. Incidentally, Keller was to become president of Dodge in 1929.

Downtown, in New York, in 1928, the consensus was:

196

Chrysler's bought a lemon. That was the opinion of some minds that contained little understanding of industry, and especially of the automobile industry. Buying the Dodge was one of the soundest acts of my life. I say sincerely that nothing we have done for the organization compares with that transaction. We had, before the merger, an intensely sharp spearhead in the Chrysler Corporation, but when we put behind it all of Dodge our spearhead had a weighty shaft and had become a potent thing. Yesterday—this is May, 1937—we built 6294 cars; the day before, we built 6500, and so it goes, in what some people still suppose is a depression. Yet, had we lacked Dodge, there is no telling what our situation would be today. For one thing, there would be no Plymouth car.

The Chrysler Corporation as of 1937 has no debts. Between the stockholders and the operating property represented by their 4,300,000 shares there is no sort of mortgage, no preferred claim. Getting rid of burdensome interest charges was just one phase of the course we pursued to come through the depression so as to emerge stronger than when it began. Who that lived through it will ever forget the beginning?

Early in 1929 it had seemed to me that I could feel the winds of disaster blowing. I had a great responsibility as a trustee. In my half year of retirement from the automobile business after leaving General Motors and selling my stock to Du Pont and Durant, I had given everything I owned to my wife and children. I put it into trusts which were made irrevocable. So, when I had gone to work for the bankers in the Willys-Overland situation, I had been a man without capital. During 1929 my family's stocks had taken the shape of cash in the banks. About the stuff I owned myself that year I was something less than smart. However, I came to the conclusion that what my boys ought to have was something to be responsible for. They had grown up in New York and probably would want to live there. They wanted to work, and so the idea of putting up a building was born.

Something that I had seen in Paris recurred to me. I said to the architects: "Make this building higher than the Eiffel Tower." That was the beginning of the seventy-seven-story Chrysler Building.

The architects had made a plaster model—and in the toy-sized lobby, tinted Morocco red to simulate marble, the ceiling was supported on four free-standing columns.

"It looks a little cramped, to me," I said. Until that point I think the architects had felt I was taking rather little interest.

"A terrific load is carried by those columns in the plans as drawn."

"Um, but when people come into a big building they should sense a change, get a mental lift that will put them in a frame of mind to transact their business—how about this?" I reached my fingers through the ground floor of this skyscraper in miniature.

"Pull it out," said one of the architects. "That's just a piece of cardboard, pegged in there." I did, and that little action involving a change in the plans cost about a quarter of a million.

"Could it be done?" I asked.

One of the architects was sketching on an envelope. He held up his sketch. He said: "It could be done this way, by making the lobby triangular." Even as we made the change the steel for the subsurface part of the building was being fabricated. From that point on I had all kinds of fun; spent lots of hours down on my hands and knees creeping about the floor of my office—then at 347 Madison Avenue—

carpeted with the blueprints and the other drawings of the architects; made the final choice for the marbles in the corridors; chose the veneers that make the interior of each elevator cab seem to be the work of some extraordinarily gifted cabinetmaker.

"If the elevator cabs travel less than straight," I said to myself, "they will be more noisy than pistons in cylinders that are out of round. I want them perfect."

So I gave orders as to how the plumb lines should be taken. Today, I think, we've got the finest elevators to be found. The city laws only tolerated speeds of 750 feet a minute when we built. I insisted on preparations for speeds of 1000 feet a minute, which the law now allows. In consequence, with all the building occupied, the elevators can handle the peak-load crowd without delay. But such matters now are problems for my son, Walter. He is running the building. He is president, and he knows his job.

When he was ready to go to work, I said, "You better learn something about the building. It's yours; not mine."

"Where do you think I ought to begin, Dad?"

"Get down in the basement and learn what the other fellow's got to do. Go and scrub a few floors. Clean some offices. That way you can begin to see through the glasses of other people as well as your own." He did it, too, and then proceeded through various jobs until he was well able to run the building. That enterprise is working now as in 1929 it was planned that it should.

But you can be sure that when we started erecting that tall building I had no idea that ahead of me were the hardest, most troubled years of my life. I consider it fortunate for me that the building was practically a completed project before the awful character of the depression was revealed.

My wife and I like parties just as much as we did when we were an engaged couple out in Ellis, Kansas; we enjoy music and hearing the laughter of our friends, but as the business situation grew more disturbing she felt we should talk things over.

I told her: "If the Chrysler Corporation ever needed support, it needs it now; it needs me. So, five days a week I am going to be in bed early and I'll be up early and off to work. On Friday nights, if you like, we can go somewhere, to dinner, or a movie, or a show. But I must be in bed by midnight. On Saturdays we'll stay up as late as we like. On Sunday nights I'll be going to bed early so as to be fresh for Monday morning. That is our schedule until this thing is over."

We stuck to that faithfully. Della encouraged me. She knew she was still the wife of a workman.

Expenses of the Chrysler Corporation had to be cut during 1931, 1932 and 1933. We had to cut salaries, reduce operations, retrench in almost every way. There were bleak months when the plants, for lack of orders, were operating down to forty per cent of capacity. But no matter how gloomy the outlook, I never cut one single penny from the budget of our research department. I think Carl Breer, who runs the research, will bear me out in this. I can't recall that he was asked to stint on anything. The reason for that is something that any modern industrialist knows and understands. Its research work is what will be keeping any soundly managed industry alive and healthy five and ten years in the future. As the depression became worse, as people became more gloomy, we grew bolder in our research. The things that were developed in the laboratories in those dark days are the improvements that created a strong demand for cars in 1936 and 1937. Research is the answer, if anyone should ask why modern cars are so much improved; it is why the automobiles of the future will be incomparably better than any we have seen.

But other things of vital importance were being accomplished in our organization through the years of the depression. After we had taken over the Dodge Corporation in 1927 we had a total debt of $60,000,000; that meant we had to make $3,600,000 to meet interest charges. All of my associates were agreed that we ought to keep reducing that debt, and we did. The man who became comptroller of the Chrysler Corporation and its subsidiary companies when that debt was biggest, in 1927, is Lester A. Moehring. Mr. Moehring's job involves not only accounting and control, but also preparation of budgets and forecasts of what the business may be expected to do. Thousands of clerks are kept busy under Mr. Moehring so that he can boil out the essential figures which the Chrysler operations committee needs for its decisions. Thanks to steadily accurate knowledge of the corporation's position, we dared to pay debts until $60,000,000 of the Dodge debentures was down to $30,000,000. There came a day when, thanks to a splendid credit, we borrowed $25,000,000 at a very low rate of interest, added about $5,000,000 of our cash, and called the bonds. Finally, with some of the profits of 1934 and 1935, we got ourselves completely out of debt.

Even more important, I suppose, were the millions the corporation was spending for new equipment in the years after 1929. We began 1937 with a demand that was far bigger than our production. If we had discovered that it was desirable to remodel a plant at that time we would have been unable to stop, except at an outrageous cost. Fortunately we did not have to concern ourselves about plant improvements, because the factory layout had been made almost completely new. So our vast mechanism for producing cars came out of the depression not only free of expansion debts, but it is completely rehabilitated, almost as new and fine as a 1937 car.

But there is more to industry than money and machines. There are men. I worked too many years on account of my own family to be forgetful that it is for their women and children that men keep on working. As of 1937 there were 76,000 people on the payrolls of the Chrysler Corporation. Can it be supposed by anyone who knows me that I am unmindful of that obligation? How could I be when I am so proud? Just as I used to see my father's locomotive as the machine that gave us a living, so I now see and understand this enterprise I've helped to build as a more magnificent and infinitely more intricate machine giving sustenance and other services to many. You just bet I'm jealous of it. I want it to be more and more successful in its operations, in all its human relationships; but no matter how proud I feel because it bears the name of Chrysler, I never fool myself that I did all this. Is our engineering superb? Yes, but that is because of Fred Zeder and his associates. Has its export business flourished clear around the world? We owe that to vice-president W. Ledyard Mitchell. Any great industrial corporation lives and grows only through the devoted services of many who pool their intelligence and energy in a common effort.

I really understand it best, I think, when I go out to Detroit and sit at a meeting of the dozen younger fellows who are running the business. I am a sort of grandsire there, the chairman of the board. I got my start in overalls; so did Keller, the corporation's president; so did Zeder; so did Hutchinson; so did Skelton; so did Breer; so did Mitchell; so did Byron Foy; and so did many of the others. We are, all of us who sit at that table, American workmen in the simple, exact meaning of the term. Those who come after us in the years ahead will be the same, and the reason for this is that there is no way for men to qualify themselves for what we do at that table except by work and learning.

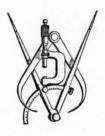

A POSTSCRIPT

TWELVE years have passed since any further conversations with Walter Chrysler might have been arranged. On May 26, 1938, he became ill and never regained his health. He died August 18, 1940. Obviously his own story of his life has to end just where he left it. Yet there is much more to say about such a man. And it should be said.

His grandchildren and all of their generation on this continent shall live as free beings on this Earth only if those Americans Walter Chrysler typifies are left free to make things to the best of their abilities.

They do not occur numerously. Unhappily we have no single enlightening word to distinguish the rare kind of leadership for which Walter Chrysler had been struggling to qualify himself in an amazing sort of apprenticeship after he had completed his machine shop apprenticeship.

This son of Kansas pioneers, born in the vastness of the Western plains, never allowed himself to forget that ours has been the only nation thus far to span and prosper on a continent. This happened in North America only by means of mechanized transportation; first the railroad, then the automobile. Even now we are—or hope we are—in the process of making a greater nation by means of the airplane. Although he is remembered as a great manufacturer of automobiles, this American thought of himself as a "transportation man." Maybe there was a strain of this in his blood. But he took scant interest in a genealogical researcher's report that he had a sea-going Dutchman among his forebears; one Captain Jan Gerritsen Van Dalsen; that in 1622 a Dutch mariner with this name had been in the New World, exploring a nameless stream, afterwards called the Hudson, with a fleet of ships. As to that, Walter Chrysler made it plain to me he was in accord with Jimmy Durante: "Ancestors? I got millions of 'em!"

Since Walter Chrysler died, however, he is seen to have developed a power of understanding transcending transportation and utterly vital to the further existence of the people of the United States of America. He had created an outstanding institution among those companies which, when challenged, made literally anything our country needed to withstand and overwhelm the enemies that were assaulting it. This is genius; so if we are ever to comprehend our nation's strength and support it with our votes, we must coin a better word than "manufacturer" to specify the kind of American workman Walter Chrysler had become.

During scores of centuries nations have made heroes of their victorious military leaders, with the result that always there have been ambitious youths struggling to qualify themselves for such distinction and honor. However, since World War II, it is plainly to be seen that valor alone is not enough. Except for the power of America to out-produce her enemies, the only valid heroes alive today would be generals and admirals of Germany and Japan. There is no need to be less grateful to military heroes. There is no sudden need to make heroes of our manufacturers.

Yet certainly there is desperate need in this Republic for a much better and a much wider comprehension of how all that we cherish as Americans depends on keeping the ways to advancement for the young free and unrestricted. Not the young workmen alone, however.

Consider the situation of Walter Chrysler when he left General Motors Corporation at the beginning of 1920. In the preceding three and a half years, that company had paid him substantially more than $2,000,000. Obviously no ordinary reward could have lured him out of retirement after only a few months' rest. He was really a free man, one free to do as he liked, and he liked to play as much as anyone. Moreover, he knew how to play. He loved music, hunting and fishing. He was willing to stay up half the night with friends and then go out and shoot ducks. Already he had discovered the excitement that is savored by an understanding patron of the arts.

"Why should I go back?" This was the question he propounded to the two men who were urging him to solve a problem. The Willys-Overland Company in 1921 was "in terrible shape." The $50,000,000 banks had loaned the company might be lost, but, in the sight of a man comfortably retired, what of that? Finally, when urging and imploring continued, Walter Chrysler made his proposition: $1,000,000 a year, net, for two years. This, of course, led on to the reorganization of Maxwell and the birth of the Chrysler Corporation in 1925.

But suppose the 1950 scheme of taxation had been in force in that time, especially those provisions of it which limit radically the income any individual may receive. What then? To me, at least, it seems most unlikely that Walter Chrysler would then have exposed his established reputation to great risks of failure. There would have been *no* Chrysler Corporation. The whole automotive industry would be poorer and less effective now if during the preceding quarter of a century it had lacked the stimulus provided by the aggressive and imaginative competition of Walter Chrysler's company.

In the last 25 years the Chrysler Corporation has enriched the economy and enlarged tax collections far beyond the $872,-000,000 which it has paid directly in taxes. Yet this huge sum of taxes, by itself, argues overwhelmingly against imposing a destructive load of taxation on that which makes for individual incentive. Furthermore, a much larger volume of taxes surely poured into government coffers out of the $10 billions spent for materials, supplies and services; also out of the $3 billions spent for wages and salaries and the $434 millions of dividends. The $14 billions of net sales likewise represent a vast tax gain. Walter Chrysler sometimes expressed satisfaction because every time he and his associates made a truck they made—potentially—a job for someone who would drive the truck. Just as certainly, however, each one of the thirteen million vehicles produced by this company since it began was a tax producer for as long as it was kept in operation. Therefore, it does seem short-sighted of us as a people to damper down with confiscatory taxes the ambitions of our undeveloped Chryslers.

Whether it makes sense or not, after 1920 Walter Chrysler was working for his family just as certainly as he had worked mainly on their behalf before 1920. This is why I think the place he chose for the enshrinement of his chest of tools—the tower of the Chrysler Building—was peculiarly appropriate. With those tools that he had made himself, he had "qualified" himself for the machinist's craft. Then, as a journeyman machinist, he was qualified for marriage.

He had an immense pride in the prowess of the Chrysler Corporation, but the Chrysler Building in New York City was strictly and peculiarly a work of love. "It belongs to the kids," he said to me one time. "I haven't got a nickel in it." For him, the building—certainly at times—symbolized his feeling for his family's security just as surely as in earlier times similar feelings found expression in the block house of a frontier settle-

ment. Nevertheless, the other institution named for him, The
Chrysler Corporation, is now revealed as vastly more important
to the real security of his family and of all other American
families. The war was to give even a greater meaning to his
life than I, for one, had seen; and I say this believing I had
seen with fair understanding how wonderfully the meaning of
America had been revealed in his adventures.

Obviously money alone never had been the main spring
driving him. In his boyhood he had been passionately eager
to excel and as a man and a machinist all his adventures were
flavored by that same passion. On his way up he had been constantly concerned to qualify himself for some bigger field of
opportunity, yet always with machines. The creation of the
Chrysler Corporation was a logical accomplishment of Walter
Chrysler's life. Actually, of course, a manufacturing company
is itself a gigantic mechanism; one consisting of myriads of
lesser mechanisms that can be fancifully likened to the assemblage of musical instruments required for the production of
symphonic music. Without musicians, of course, the instruments are useless things. But even when instruments and
musicians are properly conjoined they would produce noise
rather than music except for their conductor. Happily, the
Chrysler concept of a well organized manufacturing company
took account of the inevitable and constant need to replace
machines and leaders.

It seems to me he had brought it to a point of excellence by
1937 and that year, in one of our last conversations, he had said
he was no longer to be thought of as one of the men running
the business. "Me? I'm just watching it," he said. He certainly was doing that.

One day after our work was finished and had been published
in the *Saturday Evening Post,* he undertook to make me see
how satisfying for him the actual response had been—and how

surprising. Outside his office I had been shown an array of letters making a bulk of several cubic feet and someone there had estimated 7000 had been received. More were coming with each delivery of mail. Nevertheless, even after the first issues of the magazine were off the press he had been sorely worried.

But for any delays and discomfort I had been subjected to because of his forebodings he was apologizing. He wasn't being mealy-mouthed about it, either. He said: "I know I was difficult to get along with—and you were so patient!" This was not flowing entirely from a sense of justice. He was trying to make me be the first to re-introduce a subject on which he himself had laid a taboo. My curiosity, however, had been freshly excited by a more recent taboo that had scarcely any importance to me. I had been told he had made bitter objections when he learned the magazine series was to be advertised by one sheet posters in the subways, at railroad stations and in other places where newsstand sales might be increased. Why had he objected?

"I was scared," he said.

"Of what?"

"Workingmen! They might go and write on those signs." Then, seeing I was still bewildered, he made a further effort to explain. That time he succeeded as if by a lightning flash. "Like a horse out on the road without blinders, I see too many things."

I should have understood without his explanation. For one thing, he was sensitive or, as he would have said, "touchy." But the important thing that made him so in this instance was his immense responsibility. Most of us have nothing comparable in our own lives to that gigantic engine which had taken on life and grown so wonderfully under his ministrations.

The other taboo referred to was a book; that is, *this* book which now appears thirteen years after the contents originally were printed in a magazine.

The project had begun in August, 1936, with George Horace Lorimer, the editor of the *Saturday Evening Post;* not with Mr. Chrysler. I was dubious. Several close associates of Mr. Chrysler had assured me that later on it might be possible to get his consent and cooperation, but among them the consensus was that it would be useless to make such a proposal just then; further, that to try and fail would prejudice any attempt made in an otherwise auspicious time. So I had tried to interest Mr. Lorimer in somebody else's story and then he took pains to show me he really wanted the Chrysler story. Commonly a free lance was concerned to sell him. This time the editor was striving to sell me.

The really astonishing thing to me was another aspect of the matter. Previously I had discovered that as a market for such wares as I brought to him Mr. Lorimer was quite uninterested in the lives of automobile manufacturers. Seemingly it was believed that if the story of one was printed this might antagonize all the others. I had made that discovery one time when I had been rash enough to suggest there *ought* to be a story in Chrysler. But having changed his mind, Mr. Lorimer proceeded to itemize the reasons why the Chrysler story could be outstanding. For one thing, there was the Chrysler Building which had been, briefly, tallest in the world. Further, there were millions of automobiles on the streets and highways of the nation. Every car quadrupled the challenge to curiosity. On each of four chromiumed hubcaps the name Chrysler was inscribed. Clearly it was a name as provokingly mysterious as that of the Count of Monte Cristo. Mr. Lorimer mentioned other reasons that seemed to increase journalistic value by tending to increase curiosity. The editor exposed the core of his enthusiasm when he spoke of the way Mr. Chrysler had strengthened his company during the depression. Then, however, Mr. Lorimer, in disclosing why a Chrysler story "later on" did not suit him, filled me with dismay: he confided that he had decided to retire. He said: "I want this Chrysler series to run as the last story of a business man's success to appear in the *Post* under my editorship." On top of that he offered to write a letter of introduction for me. So, after sending a telegram to Mr. Chrysler requesting an appointment, I had gone back to New York; and Mr. Chrysler, after reflecting a few minutes, scribbled on Mr. Lorimer's letter: "Hello, Old Top. I'll go along with Mr. Sparkes."

I was mightily pleased then. But several months later there had been a change. Even after thirteen years my unhappiness seems justified. I had found myself out on a limb further than I should care to go again in such a free-lance venture. Except for a brief bit of writing that could be done effectively only by the other party to the collaboration, the Chrysler autobiography was approximately five-eighths done; that is, to my satisfaction and that of Mr. Lorimer. But what I needed was a holographic endorsement somewhere on the script, a simple "O.K. W. P. Chrysler, Sr."

Unhappily for me, the time I had intended to spend on this work had been extended by many weeks because of interruptions in our schedule of appointments. Lacking his approval, my written account of what he had narrated in a series of conversations—recorded and transcribed by a stenotypist—had no status as a property in the field of letters.

I had been unable to see him for weeks at a time and then—in mid-December—there was a telephone call. "The Boss is back and has the morning free. Can you come over?"

Indirectly I had learned Mr. Chrysler had been appalled by something that might be said to infest the copy as termites in a neglected house. An awful lot of revision seemed to be indicated. Some of my impatience to see Walter Chrysler had leaked out of me when I stepped into one of those Chrysler Building elevator cabs. Indeed, I would have been content to be lifted much more slowly in the shaft of that towering structure than the 1000 feet-a-minute rise of which he was so proud.

Time and again after we began he had interrupted his narrative with an exclamation and an additional warning. The common purport of these had been that I would be making trouble for myself if I used all that he was then reciting. "I'll just take it out! I'll pencil it out!" If those admonitions had been bricks, I think I might have built of them a structure taller than the Chrysler spire.

He had freshly read most of what he had recited to me just before the day I am recalling. His private office was fixed high up in a stratum of gale incessantly blowing—it seemed—in from the Atlantic. The sound of it suggested there were poltergeist wailings just outside his window panes. He had one of the typescripts on his desk between his arms. So on that day especially I was conscious of the shrilling wind.

"Know what I want? Take all those out and stack 'em like cord wood." He was tapping with his finger where there was a circular pencil mark; what it ringed was a capital "I." "I'm afraid of all this 'I, I, I, I.' "

I felt better at once. His point was a sound and objective criticism of his story. No matter what proportion of habitual readers of autobiographies suffer from an insufficiency of Vitamin B, surely all of them get an overdose of the "I" of other men. Something was operating here in Walter Chrysler of much greater significance than at first appears.

An essential quality of his importance in our times was his expertness in organizing and directing the work of others. He never failed to be concerned for the dignity of workingmen.

Although he was frequently arbitrary and blunt in dealing with more important persons, he never let himself forget how it felt to be dressed in overalls with only a broom and cleaning rags for tools.

I remember one day a young fellow in grimy khaki was surprised by our sudden reappearance in Mr. Chrysler's private office. The man was thickly belted in the harness of his craft. He was a window cleaner, and those who clean the windows of New York skyscrapers are regarded by the insurance companies as adventurers of the first rank. These men were non-insurable not so many years ago and even today pay half again as much for ordinary life insurance as common men. This one was sullen faced as he hastily gathered up his bucket, squeegee and chamois cloth. Then Mr. Chrysler spoke to him.

"What's your hurry, Son?"

"You're busy. I'm getting out." No form of address from this independent cuss—at least not right away.

"Son, you don't have to go out. Get paid by the window, don't you?"

"Won't I bother you, Mr. Chrysler?"

"No, and if I'm bothering you, I'll use another room until you're finished."

When the window panes were clean and the man had vanished, Mr. Chrysler made a somewhat cryptic remark. "I've been a nut about that for years."

"What?"

"Taking pains to make any workman I come across know I don't think I'm better than he is. Unless I do, he will. Watch me leave here some night. I find things to say. 'It's a bad day' or 'kind of cold out' or something. I speak coming and I speak going. If the young man at the information desk on the ground floor has his back turned, I make a point of it; he's got to speak to me. I say: 'Good night, Son.' Now they all speak to me as soon as they see me!"

A more emphatic man would be hard to find and when he recalled an adventure the recital would be as exciting as the climax of a good second act. Yet all too many times the finish was followed by a sudden change of mood as he realized afresh that behind my interest was a purpose. Suddenly he would exclaim: "You can't use that one. Hurt that guy's feelings." Other times he would admonish me that a man "mustn't blow his own horn." Yet he never really concealed his true feeling that it was too bad a man can't give off tuba-like blasts now and then from such a choice body of experiences as had befallen Walter Chrysler. There was, for example, that time when the New Deal was young and N.R.A.'s blue eagle was a most aggressive bird.

"That's what's wrong with N.R.A. Made no distinction between good and bad. The rotten apples and the sound ones all dumped into the same bag. There is a lot of good business in this country; far more good than bad and that's why so many business men are against the administration."

He, incidentally, was *not* against it. But he was deeply proud of the company that bore his name, proud of the people making their living in its employment, proud of the products. Dangerously ugly propaganda against business—any and all business—had been coming out of Washington as molten lava from an erupting volcano.

It was William C. Durant who told me about the time Walter Chrysler was in a conference room in a Washington hotel together with other leaders of the automotive industry, striving to establish a workable "code" under which they could go on making automobiles. Then General Hugh Johnson appeared among them. He was acting tough. He was going to make everybody sign. "Make," he said, as if he alone spoke with the voice of the U. S. A.

Concerning Hugh Johnson, among business men then, the common opinion was that he seemed tough, rude and profane. Very suddenly the face of Walter Chrysler was close to the face of Hugh Johnson and the hand of Walter Chrysler, with fingers widely spread, was on the shirt bosom of the chief of N.R.A.

"Sit down, you gold braided so and so," he said. Then he pushed and Hugh Johnson sat down with a grunt. Thereafter he listened for quite awhile. All things considered, he heard a quite rational and well tempered argument.

"Get everybody in the United States thinking business in this country is bad just because it is business, and you know what? Sure as Hell we'll have a revolution. If government starts running all business and industry it has to run the people. Run everybody. That's the danger. Bad as some business is, all the danger is on the government side."

After *that* part of the session was over, the meeting marked a gain for N.R.A. Everybody felt better. The General thereafter addressed the manufacturer as "Walt" and the manufacturer, with matching courtesy, called him "Hugh."

Walter Chrysler's leadership in the Chrysler Corporation did not end when death vacated his place as chairman of the board of directors; and it is far from being ended yet. The best witness to an aspect of this influence is K. T. Keller, the president of the Corporation. Shortly before the tenth anniversary of Mr. Chrysler's death, Mr. Keller said: "Often I would be puzzled if obliged to say what we have reasoned out for ourselves when a major decision has been made during the last ten or twelve years and what has resulted from heeding certain cardinal principles of Walter Chrysler."

One continuing policy about which Mr. Keller is not in the least puzzled is the Corporation's rate of growth. A time came when these two, with many disastrous cases of industrial over-expansion in mind, made a kind of pact never to tolerate expansion of the Chrysler Corporation more than ten per cent in any year. That, however, was after an adventure in which the Chrysler Corporation had established an expansion record by becoming suddenly five or six times its former size. This was done to achieve a peculiar dimension which the people of the Earth who still are free desperately need to comprehend.

As its corporate life began in 1925, the Chrysler Corporation ranked No. 32 in the automotive industry measured by annual production. Only a few years later it was producing more automobiles than any other company except General Motors Corporation. To some extent this change had been wrought by adding to Chrysler the immense manufacturing and marketing facilities of the business the Dodge brothers left their heirs and which had been sold to bankers. One time Mr. Chrysler said to me: "The greatest thing I ever did was buy the Dodge." It was great because thereby he got for the Chrysler Corporation what might be thought of appropriately as the essential tool of volume production. By putting Chrysler and Dodge together, Mr. Chrysler had made a manufacturing organization not merely bigger, but as he said, "big enough." By this he was emphasizing that the company had been big enough to apply the full benefits for volume production of our gigantic American market. This was the crucial lack that had caused him in 1920 to be so sure that Citroen, a French automobile manufacturing company, had no proper place in the General Motors organization. Citroen was limited by the frontiers of France, by all the customs barricades of Europe. Now, thirty years later and after another World War, adjustment of this same gigantic fault in the economy of Europe has become a major goal of our foreign policy. A great part of what we strive to buy with Marshall Plan funds is a Western Europe made strong as the United States is strong. America is potent productively because it is a unified market challenging to the utmost the ingenuity of American manufacturers.

Without the great volume which exists potentially in a great market there might be reason to deplore great size in a manufacturing company. But size is vitally necessary if a manufacturing company is to produce such things as Chevrolets, Fords and Plymouths.

This is an elemental fact about our outstanding strength as a nation. Yet it has been applied with great effectiveness thus far only because in our past we had unquestioning faith in a form of government founded on the rights of individuals. In recent years there has been much preaching with the lips about the free enterprise system and much sinister practice tending to destroy that system.

Although an invalid, Walter Chrysler was still alive at the time of Dunkirk; that was when the war began for America, the end of May, 1940. Pearl Harbor, a year and a half later was simply an unmasking of hideous enemies already recognized. At the start of 1950 we seemed to be waiting again to be surprised by a recognized enemy. On this account, it is appropriate to consider the catastrophic affliction we may fix on ourselves through our succession of witless surrenders to Socialists. Socialism is the antithesis of the order under which Walter Chrysler evolved.

Think how greatly our production for the armed forces would have been affected during the last war had this American never been tempted out of Ellis, Kansas. Indeed, imagine the gain for our enemies in the last war if in 1925 they had somehow managed to discourage Walter Chrysler from proceeding with the formation of the Chrysler Corporation. Who can say what we might *not* have been able to produce of all that actually was produced. Here is the war production score of the Chrysler Corporation:

25,000 Tanks
18,000 Wright B-29 Engines
60,000 Bofors Guns
5000 B-29 Fuselage Assemblies
29,000 Marine Engines
10,000 Corsair Landing Gear
30,000 Fire Pumpers
300,000 Rockets
360,000 Bomb Shackles
12,000,000 Duraluminum Forgings
435,000 Army Trucks
12,000 Tank Engines
5500 Curtiss Helldiver Center Wings
2000 Radar Antenna Mounts
5500 Sperry Gyro Compasses
3 billion rounds—Small Arms Ammunition
100 miles of Submarine Nets
1586 Searchlight Reflectors.

Every time we had a conversation, it seems to me, he shed tears yet always what started them was thinking of the past when he was a poor young man. Sometimes, at first, I mistakenly supposed that he was feeling sorry for himself. Finally I came to realize what it was that so deeply moved him when he contemplated his inauspicious start, including those years of riding freight trains from town to town when he was hunting a chance to work and gain more experience. It was gratitude, of course; gratitude to everything American that made possible his great success. He told his story in the hope it might inspire other lonely boys roving in the land to keep on trying.